SOMALI-ENGLISH
ENGLISH-SOMALI
DICTIONARY AND PHRASEBOOK

NICHOLAS AWDE,
CABDULQAADIR XAAJI CALI XAAJI AXMED
and MARTIN ORWIN

HIPPOCRENE BOOKS
New York

Thanks to Fred Hill for his support and creative input.

Hippocrene Books, Inc
171 Madison Avenue
New York, NY 10016

ISBN 0-7818-0621-6 (pbk.)

Typesetting by Nicholas Awde/Desert♥Hearts

Printed in the United States of America

CONTENTS

- A Somali person is a **Soomaali**.
- The adjective for Somali things is **Soomaali**.
- The Somalis call themselves **Soomaalida**.
- The Somali language is called **Af Soomaali**.
- Somalia is **Soomaaliya.**

INTRODUCTION

Somalia was known in ancient times as the fabled land of Punt, the biblical place known to the Egyptians for its incense and herbs. In a later age, the British explorer Richard Burton was to describe the people of Somalia as a "fierce and turbulent race of republicans" — and, indeed, the Somalis have always retained an ethnic and cultural distinctiveness despite centuries of Arabian influence and a long history of partition of their land, situated as it is at the strategic mouth of the Red Sea leading to the Suez Canal. The nations of Britain, France, Italy, Egypt, Ethiopia and Kenya have all, at one time or another, administered parts of 'Greater Somalia' and the reunification of the Somali people has remained high on the national agenda since independence in 1960.

Somalia is one of the most ethnically homogeneous states in Africa — and all the groups there which are ethnically Somali share a common cultural background, but there are still wide differences between the pastoral groups and the sedentary peoples. In a country severely affected by drought and war as well as the long-term effects of massive foreign aid and foreign debt, it is presently difficult to estimate the total Somali population. Perhaps there are around five to eight million, excluding another million living abroad as migrant workers or refugees. Aside from Somalia itself, Somalis have also traditionally lived in Kenya's North-West Frontier province and Ethiopia's Ogaden Desert. This has been subject to much change in recent years, however.

Aside from the traditional ways of herding livestock — mostly camels, sheep and goats — and trading along the coast, an important source of employment for many Somalis is as migrant workers in the oil sector of the neighboring Arab states. It has been estimated that as many as 250,000 at any one time work there, in the process providing a significant part of Somalia's economy. It is hoped that local sources of natural gas and petroleum will be located and developed in order to create new employment as well as break the present reliance on energy imports.

Islam spread to the Horn of Africa in the 9th and 10th centuries as the Arabs came to settle in the ports along the coast. The 12th century saw waves of migration southwards from the north by Somali clans who occupied the general area they occupy today, and the region bustled with their trade, mingled with the movements of pastoralists and their herds. By the 16th century, the Somalis had already hit the history books when Ahmed Gurey, one of their clan leaders, led an army of fierce warriors on a *jihad* or holy war against the neighboring Christian kingdom of Ethiopia.

The 15th and 16th centuries saw the arrival of the Portuguese, who sought to control Somali trade, particularly in the south. After two centuries of this European presence along the coast, the Omani Sultanate then took over from the early 18th century and held onto the reins of trade until colonialism in the late 19th century started its relentless carving up of the African continent.

First the Egyptians took over the coastal towns, then the British, who had made a commercial presence as early as 1827, linked Aden, on the other side of the Red Sea, with Somalia as a suitable base for monopolising trade in the Indian Ocean. Their desire for full political control soon followed.

By the 1880s, Somali clan leaders had signed protectorate treaties with Great Britain, but many other groups fought strenuously against foreign domination, significant resistance ending only well into the second decade of the 20th century. Notable was Seyyid

Mohamed Abdille Hassan (unfairly dubbed the 'Mad Mullah' by the Western press), who headed a *jihad* against the 'infidel' colonisers — particularly the Ethiopians and the British — for almost 20 years.

By the late 19th century the French had also started to make inroads into Somalia — as had the Italians, who saw the southern region as essential to building an empire that included the ancient kingdom of Ethiopia. But the Italian incursion into the Horn of Africa backfired and their military defeat sparked a counter-expansion by Ethiopia which claimed the (then) Somali Ogaden for its own and threatened the French and British protectorates in the north.

At the end of the Second World War, however, the British were given control of Italian Somaliland as well as the Ogaden until 1950. Once more Somalia was divided up again, with Southern Somalia reverting to Italy and the Ogaden to Ethiopia. Under United Nations auspices, independence was eventually negotiated for the British and Italian Somalilands.

On 26th June 1960, British Somaliland became independent and on 1st July of the same year so too did Italian Somaliland. After a brief, heated debate, they were instantly re-united as a single, independent nation: the independent Republic of Somalia. French Somaliland, however, had to wait almost two decades more for its own independence (see below).

But conflict was never far away. The year of 1963 saw Somali insurrection in Ethiopian-held Ogaden, fired by the unification of the Somalilands, while a five-year guerrilla campaign began in an attempt to gain independence for Somalis living in Northern Kenya.

After a brief period of democracy under civilian rule, General Mohammed Siad Barre took control of the new nation he called the Somali Democratic Republic. He swiftly implemented his system of 'Scientific Socialism', backed by the USSR — in the process nationalizing much of the economy. All land came under state ownership and was leased to farmers, while in 1973-74 the National Literacy Campaign was launched to implement the new Somali alphabet — the one used in this book. But despite its Socialist bloc links, Somalia drew closer to the Middle East and North Africa by joining the Arab League in 1977.

By the same year, however, Siad Barre's policies had reduced Somalia's economy to chaos. The drought of 1974-75 had already sparked a huge influx of refugees from Ethiopia and caused internal chaos, none of which was helped by the collectivization of agriculture and fishing. In the same year French Somaliland (later renamed French Coast of Afars and Issas) became the Republic of Djibouti under the presidency of the Somali Hassan Guleid.

In order to distract attention from his country's worsening situation, Siad Barre sent army units to help Somali-sponsored rebels to try to take over the Ogaden, taking advantage of an Ethiopia weakened by the revolution against the Emperor Haile Selassie. But the Ethiopians called in the Cubans and the following year the Somali troops retreated, incurring heavy losses. The war and subsequent drought forced out even more Somali refugees who lived in the Ogaden. It is estimated that almost a million of these fled to an already strained Somalia.

Sections within the clan system moved to take advantage of the divided nation. Rioting and a failed coup led to brutal repression by the government. But this provoked the rise of a movement of rebel groups who eroded government power over the next decade. In 1991 they finally captured the capital Mogadishu.

The rebel groups failed to unite and Somalia was split once more as the north, which had previously been British Somaliland, broke away and proclaimed itself the Somaliland Republic. Meanwhile, in the south, a bitter power struggle broke out in the streets of Mogadishu between the two camps of Ali Mahdi Mohammed and General Mohammed Farah Aydeed.

The intensity of the conflict and the scale of famine were such that first the U.S. sent in troops uninvited and then the U.N. followed, in a heavy-handed attempt to impose peace. While there, this military force also took over the responsibility for ensuring the distribution of food aid to people during a famine which cost the lives of as many as 500,000. Still, the entire operation was expensive and not without controversy. The last soldiers were withdrawn in 1995, leaving behind them a continuing situation of conflict and ravaged economy, unaltered by the subsequent death of Aydeed.

The years of partition, war, civil war, foreign debt, drought and famine have taken a predictable toll on the Somali people and their land. But they have maintained a remarkable sense of nationhood throughout the recent upheavals, and this spirit has never been abandoned in the many migrant and refugee communities of the diaspora.

Somalis, wherever they may be, hope for the restoration of peace and to be given the chance to peacefully restore and reconstruct the culture, institutions and economy of their homeland.

A VERY BASIC GRAMMAR

Somali belongs to the Cushitic family of languages, which forms part of the Afroasiatic group of languages. Other members of the family include Oromo (spoken in Ethiopia and Kenya) and Afar (spoken in Ethiopia, Eritrea and Djibouti).

Somali has been written in an official script since 1972, but was written according to a variety of alphabets prior to that.

WORD ORDER

While totally unrelated to English, the structure of Somali is nevertheless quite simple. Word order is flexible, but the verb is usually put at the end of the sentence, e.g.

Shaleyto bariis waan cunay.
'I ate rice yesterday.'
(literally: 'Yesterday rice I ate.')

NOUNS

As with many other languages, like Italian, German and Arabic, Somali divides words up according to gender, i.e. whether they are masculine or feminine. This can be predictable, e.g. **naag** 'woman' (feminine) and **nin** 'man' (masculine); or not, e.g. **jariidad** 'newspaper' (feminine) and **gaadhi** 'car' (masculine). Verbs agree according to this gender, e.g.

Feminine: **Naag-tu way tagtay.**
'The woman went.'
Masculine: **Nin-ku wuu tagay.**
'The man went.'

Somali has no real word for 'a' or 'an' — just the word by itself is sufficient, e.g. **raydiiyow** means 'radio' or 'a radio.' As in, again, Italian, German and Arabic, 'the' changes according to gender: **-ka** for masculine nouns and **-ta** for feminine nouns, e.g. **dukaan** 'shop' — **dukaanka** 'the shop,' **galab** 'afternoon' — **galabta** 'the afternoon.' Note however that these forms are not fixed and can undergo a variety of sound changes.

Plurals — There are a variety of forms for the plural in Somali, and these should best be learnt with the singular of each new word you learn. Some involve a simple change of ending, e.g. **naag** 'woman' — **naago** 'women,' while others have different forms, e.g. **ilig** 'tooth' — **ilko** 'teeth,' **jariiad** 'newspaper' — **jaraa'id** 'newspapers.'

A strange feature of Somali is that often a word swaps its gender as it changes from singular to plural, e.g. **naag** is feminine in the singular but the plural **naago** becomes masculine. The reverse happens with with **inan** 'boy' which is masculine but becomes feminine for **inammo** 'boys.' At first sight it is not a predictable phenomenon, but remember that this gender reversal is a purely grammatical phenomenon.

Case — In addition to the plural, nouns in Somali also take other endings with have grammatical function, depending on where they appear in a sentence. These are best left for more advanced study, but for a note on the Vocative, see the note on page 132.

Like English, there are two ways in Somali of expressing possession, either using the Genitive: **guriga Jawaahir** 'the house of Jawahir/Jawahir's house'; or using a shortened form of the possessive pronouns: **Jawaahir gurigeeda** 'the house of Jawahir/Jawahir's house' (lit: 'Jawahir her house').

ADJECTIVES

Adjectives in Somali come after the noun, e.g.

weyn 'big'	—	**gaadhi weyn** 'big car'
yar 'small'	—	**gaadhi yar** 'small car'

Common adjectives are:

weyn big	**ladan** healthy
yar small	**wanaagsan** good
dheer long; tall	**xun** bad
gaaban short	**fudud** light; easy
quruxsan beautiful	**kulul** hot

PREPOSITIONS

Prepositions in Somali are really 'prepositional phrases' which have two forms — masculine (**-iisa**) and feminine (**-eeda**) — that agree with the gender of the noun they follow:

debeddiisa/-eeda out
gudihiisa/-eeda in
hortiisa/-eeda in front of; before
dabadiisa/-eeda behind; after
agtiisa/-eeda near
geestiisa/-eeda by
dartiisa/-eeda because of
dushiisa/-eeda on
hoostiisa/-eeda under
dhexdooda* among

But the sense of English prepositions is more often rendered by 'preverbs' (see below in Verbs).

PRONOUNS

As with verbs (see below), there are many different forms of pronouns depending on how one wants to stress the situation. However, a good basic set of personal pronoun endings (here combined with **waa**, which is often used with verbs) is as follows:

* This is a plural form.

SINGULAR	PLURAL
waan I	**waannu** we *exclusive*
waad you *singular*	**waynu** we *inclusive*
wuu he; it	**waydin** you *plural*
way she; it	**way** they
la one; someone	

Note that there are two forms for the single English word 'we.' The exclusive **waannu** means 'us only (and not the person you are talking to),' while the inclusive **waynu** means 'us all.'

'Him/her/it/them' are not translated — Somalis know the context always makes it clear what or who is being spoken about and there's never any confusion. Basic forms for object pronouns are:

SINGULAR	PLURAL
i me	**na** us *exclusive*
	ina us *inclusive*
ku you *singular*	**idin** you *plural*

Possessive pronouns have modified forms (masculine takes **k-**, feminine **t-**) which agree with the gender of the person or thing possessed:

SINGULAR	PLURAL
kayga/tayda my	**kayaga/tayada** our *exclusive*
	keenna/teenna our *inclusive*
kaaga/taada your *singular*	**kiinna/tiinna** your *plural*
kiisa/tiisa his; its	**kooda/tooda** their
keeda/teeda hers; its	

e.g. masculine **dalkooda** 'their country'
      feminine **lacagtooda** 'their money'

Demonstratives behave like possessive pronouns, and in the singular have masculine (**k-**) and feminine (**t-**) forms:

SINGULAR	PLURAL
kan/tan this	**kuwan** these
kaas/taas that	**kuwaas** that

VERBS

The structure of Somali verbs is different in quite a few ways from English. In theory the system is very logical — in practise, because of the many different endings, it may seem all a little bewildering at first. It is worth spending a little time sorting out the concept and then you will have little difficulty — Somali can be complex at times, but it's not really complicated!

Essentially the Somali verb system is an extremely flexible one that gives you a wide choice of word combinations to say what you want. First of all, every Somali verb has a basic form to which are added endings that convey information about who is doing what and when, e.g.

keen	bring!
keen-i	to bring
keen-aa	I bring
keen-ee	I would bring
keen-ay	I brought
keen-ay-aa	I am bringing

In addition to the prepositions listed above, Somali uses 'preverbs' — simple prepositions that add to a verb's meaning:

u to; for	**ku** at; in; by
ka from; about	**la** with

These are very broad in meaning and stay close to the verb, connecting with other words in a sentence, e.g.

Gabadhu laybreeriga way <u>ku</u> qortaa.
'The girl writes <u>in</u> the library.'
(lit: 'The girl the library she <u>in</u> writes.')

Note that English splits prepositions too (although for

different reasons), in sentences like 'What library did the girl write in? (lit: 'In what library did the girl write?').

When these prepositions are combined with pronouns or other prepositions they are written as one word and sometimes show sound changes, e.g. **caanaha koobka buu iigu shubay** 'he poured the milk in the cup for me' — where **iigu** is made up of **i** 'me,' **u** 'for,' and **ku** 'in.'

The negative is formed by putting **ma** 'not' (or forms combining with it) before the verb. **Ha** 'do not' is used with commands.

ESSENTIAL VERBS

Five important irregular verbs to watch out for are:

yimi to come	**yidhi** to say
yiqiin to know	**yahay** to be
yiil to be somewhere	

The verb 'to have' is formed by **hay** or **hayso**, e.g.

Basaboorkaaga ma haysataa?
'Do you have your passport?'.

'Have to' or 'must' is expressed by **waa in-**, e.g.

Waa inaan tago.
'I have to go.'

PRONUNCIATION GUIDE

Somali letter	Somali example	Approximate English equivalent
a	**dal** country	*short:* p**a**t
	daar house	*long:* f**a**ther
b	**bad** sea	**b**ox
c	**cun** eat	—
d	**dad** people	**d**og
dh	**dhul** land	—
e	**eber** zero	*short:* p**e**t
	eeg to look	*long: like the* **a** *in* p**ai**d
g	**gaadhi** car	**g**et
h	**haa** yes	**h**at
i	**nin** man	*short:* s**i**t
	miis table	*long:* s**ea**t
j	**jariidad** newspaper	**j**et
k	**kulul** hot	**k**ick
kh	**khamiis** Thursday	—
l	**ladan** healthy	**l**et
m	**makhaayad** restaurant	**m**at
n	**nabad** peace	**n**et
o	**orod** to run	*short:* c**o**t
	jooji stop	*long:* c**oa**t
q	**quruxsan** beautiful	—
r	**run** truth	**r**at, *but 'rolled' as in Scottish English*
s	**saacad** hour	**s**it
sh	**shaneemo** film	**sh**ut
t	**tagsi** taxi	**t**en
u	**lug** leg	*short:* p**u**t
	tuulo village	*long:* sh**oo**t
w	**weyn** big	**w**ell
x	**xukumad** government	—
y	**yar** small	**y**et

Nothing beats listening to a native speaker, but the following notes should help give you some idea of how to pronounce the following letters.

VOWELS
The general difference in length of vowels is important, e.g. **du̱l** 'top' — **du̱ul** 'fly'; **ba̱riis** 'rice'—**Ba̱ariis** 'Paris'

CONSONANTS
Also important is the 'doubling' of consonants, e.g. **keennay** 'we bring' is pronounced very distinctly as **keen-nay** — to distinguish it from **keenay (keen-ay)** 'I bring.'

dh can be viewed as a 'flapped' **d** or **r**, depending on the speaker — either way you'll get it right. Set your mouth up to pronounce a normal **d** or **r**, but then curl your tongue right up so that the bottom part of it touches the top part of your mouth. As you then try to pronounce the original **d/r**, you will feel your tongue 'flapping' forward.

x is a more emphatic form of **h**. Take the exhaling sound you make when you've just burnt your mouth after taking a sip of boiling hot soup, push it right back into the very back of your mouth, making sure your tongue goes back too, and that should give a good approximation! [= Arabic ح]

c if you follow the same pronunciation rules for **x**, with your tongue and back of mouth all pressed up against the back of your throat, then simply change the hiss of the **h** to a sound using your vocal cords. If you're then sounding like you're being choked, then you've got it. Hint: Rather than think of **c** as a consonant, think of it as a 'vowel modifier', and when listening to a native speaker, note how it changes any vowel in its vicinity, 'pharyngealizing' the vowel, sending half the sound up the nose. [= Arabic ع]

q is pronounced like a **k**, but right back in your mouth at the throat end, in the same area as **c** and **x**. Imagine you have a marble in the back of your throat and that you're bouncing it using only your glottis, and make a **k** sound at the same time. [= Arabic ق]

kh is the rasping 'ch' in Sottish 'loch' and German 'ach'. It is also pronounced like the Spanish/Castillian 'jota'. [= Arabic خ]

' is what is called the 'glottal stop'. You simply close the glottis at the very back of mouth/top of your throat, and then release the built-up air. The result is a light 'uh' sound with a very slight grunt just before it. Although it's not written, it occurs in the conversational speech of nearly all English speakers, being most noticeable in the pronunciation of words like "bottle" as "bo'el" by many Londoners. [= Arabic ع]

A NOTE ON SPELLING
Note that you will find variants of spellings for many Somali words — this does not reflect any significant difference in pronunciation, instead it's a situation similar to that encountered in English spelling.

THE SOMALI ALPHABET

Somali letter	Somali name of letter	Somali letter	Somali name of letter
a	[a]	m	[ma]
b	[ba]	n	[na]
c	[ca]	o	[o]
d	[da]	q	[qa]
dh	[dha]	r	[ra]
e	[e]	s	[sa]
f	[fa]	sh	[sha]
g	[ga]	t	[ta]
h	[ha]	u	[u]
i	[i]	w	[wa]
j	[ja]	x	[xa]
k	[ka]	y	[ya]
kh	[kha]		
l	[la]	'	[hamza]

SOMALI
DICTIONARY

SOMALI-ENGLISH
SOOMAALI-INGRIISI

A

abaalgud prize
aabbe father
abaar drought
abitey kite
abla-ablayn classification
abooto grandmother
abriil April
abuur xulasho seed selection
aad . . . u very
aadami human
adaa mudan! you're welcome!
adag hard; thick; difficult
addoon slave
addoonsi slavery
adduun world
adduunweyne international
  community
adeegto maid
adeegsi use
adeer (paternal) uncle
adhaxlay chordate
adhi sheep & goats
adhi-jir shepherd
adiga you
adkaysi resistance; endurance
af mouth; language
afaaf door
afar four
afar gees square
afartan forty
af-badan sharp
afeef hypothesis
afka shimbiraha beak
af-lagaado abuse
afo wife
Afrika Africa
afuuf blow
ag nearness
agagaar neighborhood; surroundings

Agoosto August
agteeda by; at the side of
ahminayn ranching
akhlaaq moral
akhri read
alaab material
alaabo ceerin raw material
alaabta wax lagu cuno cutlery
alaabo guri furniture
albaab gate; door
alkalayn alkaline
Allaah God
alle keli aamine monotheism
alleelo shell
ama or
amaah borrow
amar order
amba or
ambalaas ambulance
ammaan praise
ammaano u hayn trusteeship
aammus to be quiet
aammusan quiet
anaaniyad egoism
anshax morality
anshax xumo immorality
antaartik antarctic
antibaayootik antibiotic
aqal house
aqbal accept
aqoon intelligence; knowledge
aqoonsi recognition
arag see
aragti theory
aragti maalineed daylight vision
arbaca Wednesday
ardey student
argaggixiso terrorism
armaajo cupboard
ammin jiideed time
ammin meeleed local time

aroor morning
aroore vein
arrin matter
aasaasi fundamental
asal original
asbuuc week
aashito; aasiidh acid
ashtakee accuse
ashuun water pot
askar army
askari soldier
assalaamu calaykum! peace be with you!
astaamo characteristics
astaan mark; characteristic
atmoosfeer atmosphere
aton atom
awood authority; power
awoodda danabka biyaha hydro-electric power
awoode almighty
awood-siin jurisdiction; mandate
awoowe grandfather
awr (burden) camel
axad Sunday
axdi agreement; pact
-ay *feminine vocative suffix*
aayatiin destiny
ayeeyo grandmother
aayo ka talin; aayatashi self determination

B

-ba as well as
ba' to be destroyed
babbaay papaya
baabbi'i destroy
babbis fan
baabuur car; truck
bac (plastic carrier) bag
bacadleh market
bacrimin fertilization
bacrimiye fertilizer
bacrinnimo fertility
bad sea

badan many; much
badbaadiye fuse
Badda Cad Mediterranean Sea
bad sea
badaad survive
baadari missionary
baadariyad nun
badeeco goods
badh half
baadhis investigation
baadiye country; countryside
badhan button
badhar butter
badhax dilute
badhe equator
badhi bulb
badhtame center
badmaax; badmar sailor
badweyn ocean
bafto cotton (cloth)
bah family *of the same mother*
baahan u needing
bah cadceedeed solar system
baahid propagation; diffusion
baahin decentralised
baaji postpone; prevent
bakayle rabbit
bakteeriye bacteria
bal! oh!
balaadhan wide
balanbaalis butterfly
baal feather; page; paper
baalal wings
baalbiyood fins
baaldi bucket
baali untidy
ballanqaad promise
ballaadh width
ballaadhan wide
ballan agreement
baaluq maturation
baambad tap
bambeelmo grapefruit
bangi bank
bani aadnimo humanitarianism
baankiriyas pancreas
bannaan plain
bannaanbax protest

bannaan fatah flood plain
bannaan webiyeed river plain
bannaan xeebeed coastal plain
baansiin petrol
baqal mule
baqdin fear
baqo to be frightened
baqshad parcel
baaq (dhawaaq) announce
baaquli bowl; basin
bar teach; indicate
barabbaxin displacement
baradho; bataati potatoes
baraf ice; snow
barashada macdanta geology
barasho education; learning
baarashud parachute
barataseemolo parsley
barbaarin education; training
bare teacher
bari east; to break the day; to spend the night
baarij oats
bariis rice
barkin pillow
barkulan focus
barmiil barrel
barnaamij program
barnaaamijka (cuntada) degdegga crash (food) program
baro learn
baroosin anchor
bartame center
barwaaqo fertile land; prosperity
barwaaqo soor to prosper
barwaaqo-sooran prosperity; commonwealth
bas bus
baasaboor passport
basaasnimo intelligence; spying
basal onion
basali pink
basari untidy
basbaas chilli pepper
basbaas leh hot; spicy
baasijar passenger
basilas bacillus
baaskeelad bicycle

baasto pasta
baasto miir colander
batalaqsi paddle
batax sand
bawdo thigh; femur
bax to go; to leave
baaxad size
baxso to escape
baydhis deflection
baylin boil
bed area; field
beddel u to change; to exchange
beddelid reform
beed egg
beer farm; garden; liver; to grow; to cultivate
beeraley farmers
berberooni pepper (capsicum)
beri day; time
beeris culture (bacteria)
beeris ganaceed farming, commercial
beeritaan plant
beer kooxeed collective
beerole farmer
beer raaxo park
beerta xayawaanka zoo
beeryar spleen
beesad coin
beetalmay lavatory
bi'i destroy
bidaar bald
bidingal eggplant
bidix left
bikaac lens
bil month
bilaab; bilaw begin
biiad environment
bilaa micne nonsense
bilaydh plate
bilow start
bilowga webiga river source
biin peg; pin
biinso pincers; pliers
biqil germination
biixi-yar fibula
bir metal; iron; steel
biirbiriq to shine

bir ceeriin ore
biririf interval
birlab magnet
bir xadiid iron
birlabdanabow electromagnetism
birlaboobe magnetic
bisad cat
bisad yar kitten
bisil ripe
bislayn cooking
bislee to cook; to boil
bislow to be cooked
Bismillaah! In the name of God!
    (said before eating or drinking)
bixi to emit; to extract; to pay
bixin extraction; pay
biyo water
biyo dhac waterfall
biyo fadhiisin marshy land
biyo shub oodan inland drainage
biyo shub toosan river estuary
biyowlayda dhulka hydrosphere
bocor pumpkin
bood-bood skip
booddo flea
boodh dust; spore
boodhe brown
boodid jump
bogso (ka) recover (from)
bohol depression
boholo gullies
bool bolt
boolo stamp
boolo-boolo duck
booqasho visit
booqo visit
boqol hundred
boqor king
boqorad queen
boqortooyo kingdom; monarchy;
    sultanate
boqoshaa mushroom
boor dust
boorso bag; handbag
booskaadh postcard
boosta; boosto post office
borotiin protein
booyiso maid

burush; baraash brush
bu' nucleus
bu'da isha eyeball
buudh boot
budhcad bandit
budhcad-badeed pirate
budo flour
buufi to spray
buufin balloon
buufiye pump
buug book
buuga lagu qoro notebook
buug xasuus qor diary
buulo village
buul shimbireed nest
bulsho society
buluug blue
bullaacad drain
bun coffee
buundo bridge
bunduq gun
bunduq-madfac cannon
bunni brown
buuq noise
bur flour
buur mountain
buuran; buurnaan fat
burbur roodhiyeed crumb
burcad butter
burcad dhanaan cheese
buur duuban fold
buur fulkaaneed volcanic
buur yar hill
buuro butter
buruc belly
burus hammer
burush; buraash brush
burushka rinjiga paint brush
bus dust
buush cork
buushe bran
bushkuleeti bicycle
bushqad package
buskut biscuit
buste blanket
buux to be full
buuxi to fill

buuxso to fill up
buyaane piano
meel istaraatiijik ah strategic position

C

cab drink
caabbi resistance
cabbir measure
cabbiraad measurement
caabudid worship
cabid drink
cabsi fear
cabuudhiye piston
cad meat
cadadi coin
cadaadi press
cadaadis pressure
cadaadis beeg barometer
cadaadis fudud yar low pressure
cadaadis hawo air pressure
cadaadis wayn high pressure
cadanyo allergy
cadaw enemy
caday tooth-stick
caddaan white
caddayn; caddee to explain; to prove
cadho anger; heat; upset
cadhosan angry
cadhow to get angry
caadi usual
caadiga loo yaqaan average
caado habit
cadow enemy
caafimaad health
cag foot
caag plastic
cagaar grass
cagaaran green
cagaariye chlorophyl
cagafcagaf plow; tractor
cago feet
cajalad tape; cassette
cajiin paste

calaacal palm of hand
calaamad mark; scar; sign
calal rag
calan flag
calaykum assalaam! reply to assalaamu calaykum!
caleemo herbs
caleen leaf; herb
calool stomach
cambe mango
cammuud sand
caan universal; fame
canab grapes
cananaas pineapple
canbaruud pear
canbuur dress
candhuufo spit
canjeelo qalaad pancake
caano milk
caano diiq dairy
caano fadhi yogurt
caanoole milkman
canqow ankle
caaqil wise
caqli intelligence
Carab Arab
carar to run
cariish hut
carjow cartilage
caaro spider
carqalad barrier
carrab tongue
carro earth
carro guduud red soil
carro guur soil erosion
carro nafaqeyn soil fertilization
carro seel saline soil
carro-guur soil erosion
carro-san fertile soil
carruur children
carruusad toy
carsaanyo snail; crab
carwo fair
carwo dad circus
cas; casaan red
cashar lesson
cashee to have dinner
casho day

casri modern
casuusi pink
caato lean
caawa evening: this evening
cawaan barbaric
cawee to spend the evening
caawimo help
caws straw; grass
caws qallalan hay
cayayaan insect(s)
caymis insurance
cayn forest
cayriin raw; unripe
ceedhiin raw
ceel well
ceelka aartiis artesian well
ceeryaamo; ceeryaan fog
celcelis average
celi to return; to repeat
ceriiri dhaqaale depression (economic)
ceyriin raw; unripe
cid someone
ciid sand; holiday; festival
ciida kristmaska Christmas
ciddiyo nails
cidhib heel
cidhiidhi narrow
ciddi nail
ciddi fardood ama xayawaan hoof
cidiyo paw
cidna no one
ciidamo forces
ciidan army
cilmi intelligence
cilmiga bulshada social sciences
cilmiga tirokoobka statistics
cimilo climate; weather
cimilo-gooreed weather
cinjir rubber
cinwaan address
cir joogayaal planets
cirbad needle
cirif pole
cir sky
ciyaala suuq rascal
ciyaar dance; match; play
ciyaaryahan xirfad leh acrobat

cod sound; voice ; vote
cod dheer loud
codka boolo-boolada quack
cod muusiko note
codsi order
cudbi cotton
cudud upper arm; humerus
cudur seexiye sleeping sickness
cuf mass
cufnaanta tirada dadka population density
cufisjiidad gravity
cufnaan density
culays weight
culus heavy
cun eat
cunaqabatayn blockade
cunta qaadasho ingestion
cuntee to feed
cunto food; diet
cunto mareen alimentary canal
cunto ururin food gathering
cuntub aggregate
cunug baby; child
curad first-born child
curcur wrist
cusbataal hospital
cusbo macdaneed mineral salt
cusbo salt
cusub new; fresh; modern

D/DH

da' age; to rain
dab fire; electric
dab demis fire-engine
daba-case carrot
dabaabad tank
daabacaad print
dabadeed external
dabadeedna and then
dabagaale squirrel
dabaq floor
dabaqad class
dabargoyn exterminate
dabayl wind

dabayl joogto ah prevailing wind
dabayl ka jeed leeward
dabayl ku jeed windward
dabci behaviour
dabeecad manners
dabiici nature
dabo soco follow
dabo tail ; behind
dabool cover
dabuub discussion
dacas slipper
daciif weak
dacsad makiinadeed pedal
dacwee accuse
dad people
da'da dhulka geological age
daadguree evacuate
daad-xoor silt
dagaal fight; battle; war
dagaal sokeeye civil war
dagaal yahan jabhadeed guerrilla
daah curtain(s); cover
dahab gold
daahid lateness
daaji graze
dakhli income
dal country; pestle
daal tired
dalab order
dallaayad umbrella
daallin oppressor
dal qalaad abroad
dalag crops; input
dalag ganac cash crop
dalag gedis crop rotation
dalqo pharynx
dalool hide
dalooliye awl
dambayn backwardness
dambe behind; last; next; secondary
dambee to follow
dambiil basket
dameer donkey
dameer faraw zebra
dhammee to finish
dan interest
daan jaw
danab electrostatic

danabayn *electric* charge;
    electrification
danab qumman direct current
danabtuse electroscope
danbiil basket
danjire ambassador
daanyeer ape; monkey
daaq pasture
daaqad window
daaq cune-daaqe herbivorous
daqiiq flour; powder
daqiiqad minute
dar reason
dar ku to add to
daar house; building
daarad yard
dar isku/ku to add
darajada labaad secondary
darajo rank
dareen tension
dareenside farac xangule spinal
    nerve
dareenside waji facial nerve
dareere liquid
dariiq road; street
dariiqada loo macaamilo attitude
dariiq badeed sea route
dariiqo method
dariishad window
dameer donkey
damqasho hurt
daruur cloud(s)
daryeelid welfare
daryeelka carrada soil conservation
daa'uus peacock
daw pass
daawaadayaal audience
daawe disk
dawaco fox
dawan bell
dawaar sewing machine
dawaarle tailor
da'weyn old
dawlad state; government
dawladeed state
daawo medicine
day to look at
dayaan echo

da'yar young

daayeer monkey

day ku to try; to test

dayax moon

dayax gacmeed satellite

dayr short rains (September to November)

dayuurad aeroplane

debecsan loose

debed outside

deg to inhabit; to live; to settle; to stay

deegaan environment; vegetation

deg-deg urgent; hurry

deeqe donor

deggan living; live; stable

deg to sink

degmo community; settlement

dejin unload

deked harbour; port

derbi wall

dermo mat

deero gazelle

dhab real; lap

dhaban cheek

dhabbo lane

dhabcaal mean

dhac to drop; to fall to happen

dhadhaab rock; stone

dhadhaab dhalan rogan metamorphic rock

dhadhaab lakabeed sedimentary rock

dhadhaab shiileed igneous rock

dhadhamo taste

dhadhan taste

dhaaf pass by

dhaafi; dhaafiye pass

dhagax burbur weathering

dhakhso fast

dhakhtar *male* doctor

dhakhtarad *female* doctor

dhakhtar ilkaha dentist

dhalad indigenous

dhalaal to shine; to melt

dhalin cause

dhaliye generator

dhalo bottle; glass

dhammaad end

dhammee finish

dhan (dhamaa) to drink milk

dhanaan sour

dhaqaajiye motor

dhaqaale economy

dhaqaale fadhiid ah economic stagnation

dhaqdhaqaaq movement; activity

dhar cloth; fabric ; clothing; clothes

dharab dew

dhar ka dhig to undress

dhaw near

dhawaaq ku announce

dhawr protect

dhaxal inheritance

dhaxan cold *noun*

dhedo mist; frost

dheefsasho metabolism

dheefshiid digestion

dheeh enamel

dheel dance

dheellitiran equilibrium

dheemman diamond

dheer long; tall

dheeraad extra

dheg ear

dhegayare clove

dhegayso to listen

dheg weel handle

dheh tell

dhaqaaji move; drive

dhereran longitudinal

dhereg to be full up; to be satisfied

dheregsan full; satisfied

dheregsanaan saturation

dherer length; height

dheri pot

dheri ubaxa vase

dhex middle; waist

dhexda ukunta yolk

dhexdhexaad neutral

dhexe between; middle

dhexee to be in the middle

dhexgelid infiltration

dhex roor diameter

dhexyaal medium

dhib problem

dhib yar easy

dhibaato problem
dhibic drip
dhidib axis
dhif rare
dhibiq tiny
dhig to put down; to teach
dhigaal; dhigasho deposit
dhige longitude
dhilawyahan ivy
dhimbiil green vegetables
dhimbiliye spark plug
dhimo to die
dhin reduce
dhinac side
dhir plant; herb
dhir isku cufan hedge
dhir teel-teel ah scattered trees
dhis to build
dhismaha jugraafiga duleed physical geography
dhisme-unug cell structure
dhisid construction; building
dhogor wool; fur
dhoobo clay
dhoofi export
dhow near
dhowow to approach; **soo dhowow!** come in!
dhowr few
dhowrso (ka) refrain
dhuuban thin
dhucoyaray pint
dhufo ku hit with
dhugo peep
dhukey wax
dhukubis peck
dhul earth; land; country; ground; floor
dhul balaarsi territorial expansion
dhul bannaan field
dhulbeereed field
dhul-daaq grazing land
dhul gariir earthquake
dhulgoosi feudal
dhululubo cylinder
dhuumasho hide
dhuun pipe
dhuuni beeris subsistence
dhunkasho kiss

dhuunta faloob fallopian tube
dhusun underground
dhuux marrow
dhuxul charcoal
dib tail; rear
dibad outside; abroad
dibadeed external
dibno lips
dibqalooc scorpion
dibudhac underdevelopment
dib u habee reform
dib u hel recover
dibusocod retrogressive
diid refuse
didib limestone
diidmo refusal; resistance
difaac defence
digaag chicken
digir bean(s)
digir-cagaar peas
digrii degree
digsi pan
dil to hit; to kill
(qof) dilid murder
dimis screwdriver
diin religion; tortoise
diinlaawe atheist
dir class; send
diir peel
diirad compass
direys uniform
diriishad window
dirindiir caterpillar; worm
diirran warm; heated
diirri to heat up
disembar December
diisnaan compression
diyaar ready; prepared
diyaargarow to prepare
dood quarrel
doofaar pig
doog grass; green
doolshe cake
doollar dollar
doolli mouse; rat
doon to want; to wish; will
doondoon to look for
dooni boat

doonis

doonis want
dooni yar canoe
dooro chicken
dooro waraabe mushroom
dooxo valley
doqon silly
dub grill; skin
dubaalad filament
dubaax fresh
dubbe hammer
dube baker; oven
dub sare epidermis
ducaysi pray
duco prayer
dufan fat; grease
dugaag wild animal
dugsi school
duhur midday
dukaan shop
dukaanle shopkeeper
dukhsi fly
dul top; surface; plateau
dulin parasite
dul ka hoor rain, convectional
dulmi oppression
dulmi badan oppressive
dumar women
dun thread
duni world
dunta ciida soil texture
dun tolin thread
duray *medical* cold
durbaan drum
durdur stream
duud escarpment
duul fly
duuliye pilot
duumo malaria
duur jungle
duur joog wild animals

E

ee and
Eebbe God
eber zero

eedee to accuse
edebdarro rude
eedo paternal aunt
eeg to look; to watch
eegeeg look around
elektaron electron
engeg to dry
engegan dry; dried
ensayn enzyme
eray word
ergo ama wakiillo diin-fidineed missionary
eryo to chase
eex bias
ey dog

F

fadhiisi to sit
fadhiisi dhaqaale economic stagnation
fadhiiso to sit down
fadlan please
faafid diffusion
faag dig
faa'iido useful; profit; **(ka) faa'iidaysi** exploitation; **aan faa'iido lahayn** useless
fakiro: sida loo fakiro attitude
fal act
fallaadh arrow
faalladho rays
falfalliiran exfoliation
fallaaraha qorraxda sun rays
fallaaro rays
fandhaal *wooden* spoon
faqiir poor
far finger
faragelin intervention
faraggeli intervene
faranka budo stamp
faras horse
faras yar pony
farasmagaalo town/city center
farax to be happy

faraxsan happy
far cayeed toe
fargal ring
fargeeti fork
farmaajo cheese
faro digits
farriin message
farsamad, farshaxan craft
farshaxan artist
farshaxanyahan artist.
fursuq peach
farxad leh happy; exciting
farxad la' unhappy
faas; faash ax
fasal classroom
fasax holiday
fatah flood
fatoorad car
faxal pollen
faxal gudbin cross-pollination
faxaliid anther
faxlid pollination
fayl file
faynuus lamp
faaytamiin; faytamiino vitamin(s)
febraayo february
feedhyahan boxer
feker think
feero *flat* iron
ficil activity
fidi expand
fidid expansion
fidin extension
fidis expansion
fiidmeer bat *animal*
figta buurta peak
fiican well
fiid evening
fiidhiyoow video
fiiq sweep
fiiqan pointed
fiise visa
fiitamiin vitamin(s)
finjaan cup
fikrad thought
filfil *black* pepper
filim film
filiqsanaanta dadka population

distribution
filitaan expectation
firdhi disperse
firdhis dispersal
firdhiso diverging
firfircooni activity
firiley cereal
fishiisto fascist
fiyuus fuse
fog long; far
fogaansho distance
food forehead
foodhi whistle
foog fork
fogaansho distance
folkaaneed volcanic
foolal incisors
foolxun ugly
foormaajo cheese
foorno oven
foosil fossil
foosto barrel
footari marble
footookoobi photocopy
footoosintasis photosynthesis
forno oven
fosil fossil
frinjideer refrigerator
fritijeer refrigerator
fuud soup; food stock
fudud light; easy
fuul ride
fuuqis absorption
fur to open; to divorce
furan open
furaash mattress
fur-dabool plug
fure key
furo to open

G

gaab shortness; gap
gabay poem
gabadh girl; young woman; daughter
gaaban short

gaabis slow
gabogabo finish
gabooje cool
gacan hand; arm; handle; radius; gulf
gacanta shaadhka sleeve
gacmo-gelis glove
gad sell
gaadh to reach; to arrive
gadh chin; beard
gaadhi car; truck
gaadhi faras cart
gaadhi kiro taxi
gaadhi weyn truck
gaadiid vehicle
gaadiid badan traffic
gaadiid caafimaadka ambulance
gaadiidka hawada spaceship
gado buy
gadood anger
gaagaabiye scissors
gaajeysan hungry
gaajo hunger
gal to enter
gaal infidel
galab afternoon
galabnimo in the afternoon
galbeed west
gallay maize
galoob badh hemisphere
galool yar gut
galuus button
gal waraaqeed envelope
gambadh stool
gambo penny
ganaan malt
ganacsade merchant
ganac pancreas
ganacsi commercial
ganacsi trade
ganbaleel bell
ganjeello gate
gantaal projectile
gar aorta; chin; beard
gaar ah private
gar sambab pulmonary aorta
gaardis march
garaac to knock; to dial
garaacid knocking

garab shoulder
garan vest
garo to know; to realize
garee to do; to make
garfeedh comb
gargaar help
garoon field; ground
garoon dayuuradeed; garoon dayuuradaha airport
garsoorayaal jury
garsoore judge; referee
gaadhi qafilan van
gaas gas
gasho wear
gaatir callus
gee take
gebogebo end
gedef mask
geed tree
geed-cuf bush
geeda gooye herbalist
geedka canabka vine
geedka timirta date palm
geedo quute herbivorous
gef mistake; wrong
geftin edge
geel camels *collective*
gelid invasion
gelin invest
geeltoosiye vulture
geerash garage
geri giraffe
gees horn; side
gees careen antenna
geesi brave
gidaar wall
giraangir hoop
go' sheet; to cut
go'aan decision; resolution
go'aansasho determination
gobanimo freedom; sovreignty
goob place; side; position
goobaabin circle
gobol area; region
goborayn polarity
goob xafladeed reception; party
god hole; cave
god bahal den

godan curve
gogol mat
gogoldhig foreword
golaha la taliyayaasha advisory council
gole committee; assembly
goodi edge; hem
googooye scissors
gool goal
goolad baabuur roundabout
goomo rubber
goon tin hair follicle
goor hore early
gooryaan jillaabeed (hoog) hookworm
gooryaan mullaax tapeworm
gooryaan suun flatworm
gooy to cut
gorayo ostrich
gorgor coomaada vulture
gowdhis persecution
gows molar
goy cut
gu' long rains (April to June)
gub burn
guban burnt
gubasho fire
gubo to burn
gudbane transverse
gudbin conduction
gudin ax
gudo inside
gudo wadneed endocardium
gudub cross
guduud red
guuleyso ku succeed in
gujo impulse
guluub *electric* bulb
gumaysi dahsoon indirect rule
gumud tare nodule
gunbur pyramid
guntiino woman's dress
gunud to fasten; to knot; to pin
gurracan wrong
guri boqortooyo palace
guri cariish cottage
guri house; home
guud general

guuleysi; guul to win; success; victory
guuleyso ku to succeed in
guumays owl
guuris copy
guurso to marry; to get married
guurti jury
geddisle trader
geedo plants
gibil atmosphere
girid grid
gobol region
gorayo ostrich
gudbin conduction
gudbiye permeable
gufaacaale cyclonic rain
guluub globe

H

haa yes
hab institution
habardugaag wild animals
habaryar *maternal* aunt
habaynta (caanaha, hilibka) (milk, meat) processing
habaysan regular
habdhiska dareenwadka dhexe central nervous system
habdhis ikooloji ecosystem
habe permeable
habeen badh midnight
habeen night; evening
habeyn reform
habid permeable
habka biyo shubka drainage system
habka loo macaamilo behavior
habsan formal
habsaan late
habsame regular
haad large bird
hadal talk; discussion; to speak (**la** with)
hadal yar quiet
Haddii Eebbe yiraahdo! God willing!
haddiyad present

hadh shade
hadhaa backwardness
hadhuudh sorghum
hagaag straightness; to be straight
haagaag: waa haagaag! ok!
hagaaji to mend; to straighten
hagid orientation
rakaad frequency
hakin hold
hal female camel; one *(used with a noun when a single object is counted)*
halbawla beer hepatic artery
halbawle yare arteriole
halgan dhaqaale economic struggle
halganka dabaqadda; halgan dabaqdeed class struggle
halis dangerous
halkaas there
halkee where
hamaansi yawn
haan tank
handaraab knob
hangool hook
hani lab-faraarle mitral valve
hanti capital
hanti-goosi capitalist
hantiwadaag socialist
hanuunis orientation
harag skin; leather
harame weeds
haramcad cheetah
haro pond; lake
harqaan sewing machine
harqaanle tailor
harraad thirst
harraadsan thirsty
haro baddeed lagoon
hawada sare space
hawd forest
haweenay woman
hawl work; job; activity
hawlan busy
hawo air; gas; weather
hawo hays air bladder
hay have
hayn hold
hayso have

hayye ah!; hi!
heedheh hey!
heehaab suspension
hektaar hectare
hel find
hel ka to like; to enjoy
helid to find; to receive
helikobtar helicopter
heer rank
heerka badda sea level
heerka biyo gaadhka water table
heerkul madoorshe isotherm
heerkul sheeg thermometer
hees song; to sing
hees qaad to sing a song
heshiis agreement; pact; treaty
heyl cardamom
hiddo heredity
hiddo barasho genetics
hiimagoloobin hemaglobin
hilib meat
hilib cune meat eater
hilibleh butcher
hilib idaad mutton
hillaac-danab tiir lightning rod
hinjin lift
hoobad gradient
hodan rich
hodannimo wealth
hoggaami lead
hoggaamiye leader
holac flame
hoor liquid
hoorayn liquification
horjeed: soo horjeed to be in conflict (**ka**) with
hoormoon hormone
hoos bottom
hoose lower
hoos-u-dhac dhaqaale economic depression
hoose lower
hooseeya low
hoy home
hooyo mother
hoysiin accommodate
hor front part
hordhac preface

hore; horaad first; previous; primary; forward
horeeye first
horjeed opposite
horjeed ka soo; hortag to oppose
horumar development
horumar progress
horuscod progressive
hub weapon
hubaal sure
hubi prove
hudheel hotel
hufan accurate
hunguri throat
hunguri cad trachea
hurdo sleep
hurid sacrifice
hurud sleep
huur beeg hydrometer
huur humidity
huuris roast
hyuumas humus

I

iibi sell
iibis trade
ibriiq jug
iibso: soo iibso buy; **sii iibso** sell
idil whole
idhiyoloojiyad ideology
ido sheep
if illumination
iftiin bright
ikhlaaq manners
ikooloji ecology
il eye; spring; source
il-biyood fountain
ilaa until; up to
Ilaahay God
ilaali protect
ilaalin protection
ilays light
ilays dharaareed daylight

ilays light
ili-aragto macro
ili-ma-aragto micro
ilig tooth
iljebin; il jebis wink
ilka-cadayn smile
ilko teeth
ilkood dental
ilmee weep
ilmagaleen uterus
ilmo uur ku jira fetus
ilmo yar child
ilmo baby; child; tears
Illaah mahaddi! Thanks be to God!
imbaraaduuriyad empire
imberiyaaliyad imperialism
imminka now; just now
iimo defects
in amount; part
in yar few
ina boqor prince; princess
ina-adeer cousin
inan boy
inan son; daughter
indha-indhayn survey
indho eye
indhosarcaad magic
iniin; iniinyo seed
intii while
irbad needle
irid door; gate
is oneself
is qurxis make-up
is shareer leap
isbaageeti spaghetti
isbahaysi alliance
isbahayso to make an alliance
isburin contradiction
isbuunyo sponge; foam
isdhaafsi cayn exchange in kind
isdhaafsi exchange
isdhaafsi alaabeed exchange in kind
isdhexgal diffusion
isdiid antagonism
isgal joint
ishortaagid resistance
iska dhaaf skip

iska dhal hybrid
iska yeelyeel pretend
iska horimaad confrontation
iskaashato co-operative
isku dar add
iskudar confluence
isku dhex tuur plunge
isku dhisan composite
isku dhufo multiply
isku dubadhac resonance
isku mid same
isku siman smooth
isku xidhid join
isku day try
isku walaaq stir together
isku fac age group
iskukoob monopoly
isla weyni wacan pride
isla markaasi at the same time
islabarog convection
islis friction
isnac antagonism
Isniin Monday
isqurxis model
istaag stand
istaayshanka station
isticmaal use
isu'eg same
isugeyn add
isxaabalid hibernation
isxukun self-government
itaal intensity
ilaali (ka) refrain
itaalyar weak
iyo and

J

jaag jug
jaakeet jacket
jaamacad university
jaandi aluminum
jaarka neighbor
jab piece; to break
jaban cheap; broken
jabaq sound

jabi break
jacayl love
jadeeco measles; typhoid
jago plot; yard
jaho tilmaame compass
jalaato ice-cream
jalxad jug
janaayo january
janjeer inclination
jaranjaro ladder; stairs
jariiadad newspaper; journal; magazine
jarjar chop up
jasiirad island
jawaab answer
jawi environment
jeeb pocket
jeebis gudub cross section
jeclayso to like; to prefer
jeedi: soo jeedi propose
jeeg garee check
jenetika genetics
jeer hippopotamus
jeesad plaster
jeeso chalk
jelemad kettle
jid road
jiida zone
jiida baraflayda freezing zone
jiida dhexdhexaadka temperate zone
jiidasho attraction
jidh body
jidh-diid allergy
jiheeye compass
jiilaal dry season (December to March); winter
jiilaashin north-east tradewind
jiin gene
jiir mouse; rat
jiirar mice
jiisel chisel
jiko kiln; kitchen
jilbo joogsi kneel
jilib knee
jilicsan easy
jilicsan soft
Jimce Friday

jimidh size
jinac dulaa wasp
jinsi race; sexual
jir to be in a place; used to
jiritaan existence
jirran sick
jirrid stem; tree trunk
jirridda maskaxda brain stem
joodari mattress
joog to stay
joog dheer height
joog ekeeye contour
joogid present
joogso stop
joogto ah permanent
jokolaato chocolate
jooji to stop; to prevent
jugee knock
juul joules
Juun June

K/KH

kab shoe
ka badan more
kabadh cupboard
kabadh-buugageed bookcase
kabaal lever
kaabash cabbage
kabbo sip
kabo tole cobbler
kabriid match
kac rise
kacaan revolution
kacaanimo revolutionary
kacaankii warshadaynta industrial
    revolution
kaadi urine
kaadi u to wait; to delay
ka dib after
kadiifad carpet; mat
kaadihays bladder
kaadi mareen urethra
kafeey coffee
kaftan joke
kaah radiation

kaah-fal radioactive
kal period; pestle
kala separately
kaladh collar
kala dheer dheer uneven
kala durug qaarado continental
    drift
kala duwan different
kala duwid diversification (of
    crops)
kala furid undo
kala goysyo joints
kala jiid stretch
kala rog watershed
kala sooc discriminate
kala soocid classification
kala-dheer rough
kalajeclaysi bias
kalakaan heterogeneous
kalamaan antagonism
kala-saarid differentiation
kalasoor segregate
kal-diid repulsion
kal-gal periodic
kale other
kal huuris incubation period
kalidii tashada dictator
kalka qarsoon latent period
kalkaaliye nurse
kalkulatar calculator
kaaloori calorie
kaluumayste fisherman
kalluun fish
kaman lute; guitar
kamarad camera
kambiyuutar computer
ka mid ah one of
kan this;
kar to be able
kaaradh carrot
karaahiyo unpleasant
karaamo mystical
karaan la'aan unable
karaar cufisjiidad generator
karaya boiling
karaysalis chrysalis
kari to cook; to boil
karin boil; gap

kariye oven
karoote carrot
kaarootiin carotene
karti ability; efficiency
karti xukun authority
kashaafiito screwdriver
kasta each; every
ka taagan facing
ka tirsan belonging to; member of
kaatun ring
kaawiyad iron (clothes)
kayd savings; potential
kaydin preservation; conservation
kaydsan potential
kayn forest
kedis quiz
kee which
keeg cake
kelbad pincers
keli alone; single
keligii-taliye dictator
kelli canal; kidney
keen to bring
kexee to drive; to lead animals
khaanad shelf
khaas ahaan especially
khad ink
khajaar cucumber
khajilaad shy
khal vinegar
khalad mistake; wrong
khamiis Thursday
khariidad map
khashaafad x-ray
khatar dangerous
khiyaamo cheat
khudrad vegetable(s)
khudrad midho-cas cherry
khuraafaad superstition
khusayn relative
khuuro snore
kibis bread
kici to raise; to start up
kicid awake
kidhli kettle
kidhli-shaah teapot
kildhi kettle
kiilo; kiilograam kilogram

kimis bread
kiniin medicine; quinine
kinisad church
kinisad weyn cathedral
kiish sack
kiish haweed air sacs
kiish lacageed purse
kolay basket
konton fifty
koob cup
kooban ka comprised of
koodh coat
koofiyad hat
koolo glue
koonfur south
koor bell
kowaad primary
koox group
koox afeed linguistic group
kor top; up; body
kordhi to increase
kore upper
koreeya high
korid growth
koritaan grow
korniin: soo korniin underdevelopment
korodh increase
koromesoomis chromosomes
koronto current; electricity
korriin growth
kor saar pile
kor u bood to leap
kow one
kowaad first
kristaan Christian
ku meel gaar temporary
kubbad ball
kubbada cagta football
ku bari to spend the night in/at
kuberto bedcover
kug crown; zenith
kul heat
kulan meet
kulanti meeting
kulayl hot; heat
kul-ekeeye isotherm
kulmis focus

kulul hot
kuma who
kun thousand
ku-qasan infiltration
kuraan patella
kurdad dheer robe
kurux iris
kushiin kitchen
kursi chair; seat
kursi dheer sofa
kurtin log
ku saabsan concerning
kuul bead(s)
kuumi penny

L

la one (pronoun); with
-la' without
laba two
laba jeer twice
labaatan twenty
laaban folded
labanlaab double
laabato joint
laabbis; laabis pencil
labid interference
labisasho dress
laablaab fold
labo dhexaad space
lacag money
laace petal
laad kick
ladan; ladnaan healthy; well
laf bone; ridge
laf madax skull
lahaansho property
lahjad accent
laakiin but
laalaabid to fold
laallaad to hang
lalida cirka flying
lamadegaan desert
laambad candle; lamp
laan branch
laastiko elasticity

lawaxaad malleability
laws nut; groundnut
laxaad magnitude
laybreeri library
laydh light
leben brick
leef lick
leefleef lap
-leh with; owning
leexad deviation
leexleex wind
leexo swing
leexo u to turn to
libaax lion
libaax-badeed shark
libidh to disappear
lid opposite; anti-
lid mariid antitoxin
lid xoog xudumeed centrifugal force
lid-jidh gale antibody
lidh-gal antigen
lidsaacad wareeg anti-clockwise
ligan perpendicular
liic-liic wobble
liilan fibrous
liin lemon; lime
liin macaan grapefruit; orange
liin miiran lemonade
liinen linen
liino linen
liis list
lingax bireed *metal* nut
liq swallow
lis to milk an animal
lix six
lixdan sixty
lo' cattle
lool latitude
lool sare high latitude
loolalka dhexe middle latitudes
loos groundnuts
loox(a) wood; board; bat
lug foot; leg
luqun neck
Luulyo July
luuq lane

M

mabda' principle
macaan sweet
macaash profit
macalgad *metal* spoon
macallimadda dugsiga mistress
macallimad *female* teacher
macallin *male* teacher
macdaar weyn supermarket
macdan mineral(s)
macdan qodis mining
machad institution
macnee mean
macquul ah reasonable
macrufo acquaintance
madax bannaanaan independence
madax furasho ransom
madax head
madaxbannaan independent
madaxweyne president
madbacad printer
madbakh kiln; kitchen
maadad subject
maddiibad cooking pot
maaddinimo materialism
madhan empty; space
madhxin conservation
madhxiye current
madiibad bowl
madoobaad eclipse
madow black; dark
mafiiq broom
magaalo city; town
magac name
magool germination
magoolayaal deciduous
magudbin insulation
mahadsan thanked
mahadsanid! thank you!
majaajileeye clown
majarafad shovel; spade
majare sea route
majiire orbit
maajo May
makhaayad restaurant; teashop
makiinad machine; engine

makiinad dhar sewing machine
makiinad qubasho gudeed internal combustion engine
maktabad library
malab honey
malaha perhaps
malaa'ig angel
malax pus
malee to guess; to suppose
maleeyo la imaginary
maalgeli invest
maalin day
maalintaad dhalatay birthday
mallaay fish
malmalaado; malmalaato jam; marmalade; jelly
malqacad spoon
malyuun million
maamul culus oo cagojiid ah bureaucracy
maamule administrator
maan mind
mandheer placenta
mandiil razor
mansuun monsoon
maanta today
maqaar skin; leather
maqal to hear; hearing
maqalkarid audibility
maqan absent
maqas scissors
maqlid hearing
mar (women's) clothing; time; occasion; to pass
maar copper
maraakiib ships
maaran ka to manage without
maraq soup
marawaxad fan
mareykaan calico
mariid toxin
marinka webiga river course
marka hore firstly
markaas at that time
markab ship
markabka quusa submarine
maro cloth; material
maro-miis tablecloth

maroodi elephant
maroori to wind; to twist
maarso March
martiqaad entertain (guests)
marwo lady
mas snake
maas leather
masaajid mosque
masalle prayer mat
masar handkerchief; scarf
masax rub
mashiinka cajaladdaha record player
mashiinka cuntada shiidan food processor
mashiinka dharka lagu dhaqo washing machine
mashquul busy
masiibo calamity
masjid mosque
maskax mind; brain
maskax yar cerebellum
maskaxda dhexe mid-brain
mastarad ruler
masuuliyad responsibility
mataano twins
matiiriyalisim materialism
matoor engine
mawjad wave
maxaa; maxay what
maxbuus prisoner
maxkamad court
maya; may no
maayad current
mee where?
meeday where?
meherad work; occupation
meel place
meerada nolosha life cycle
meerayaal planets
meeshee where
meesiyan differentiation
mici sting
miici hardwood
micno-dari rubbish
mid one (used on its own when 'one' particular thing is referred to)

midab color
midab casuus orange
midabee to dye
midab samayn coloring
midabsiis pigment
midabtakoor apartheid
midayn unification; amalgamation
midee unite
miidh segregate
midhicir weyne large intestine
midhiq vanish
midho fruit; seeds
midho-cas cherry
midho madow blackberry
midig right
midow unification
migdayn tanning
milan solution
milix salt
milixsanaan salinity
minan house
mindhicir intestine
mindi knife
miinshaar saw
miiq filament
miiqlay debris
miir sieve; strainer
miridh minute
miro fruit(s)
miro dhannaan citrus fruits
miis desk; table
miisaami weigh
miisaan scales; weight
miisaan garboole balance beam
miisaan gariireed balance spring
miis dukaan counter
mise or . . . ?
misig hip
miishaar saw
miiska kaawiyadda ironing board
miskiin poor
miyaa is it that . . . ?
miyi interior of country
miyir la'aan unconscious
monoboli monopoly
moofo oven
moos banana
moqor sanbabeed pleural cavity

mooto scooter
moxoggo cassava
mooye mortar
mucaarad *political* opposition
mudac fork
muftaax key
mug capacity
mugdi darkness
muhiim main; principal
mujtamac community
mukulaal cat
muuqaal features
muraayad glass; mirror
muran quarrel
muriyad necklace
murti wisdom
murugo unhappiness
muruq muscle
muus banana
mushahaar pay
mushahaaro salary
mushkilad problem
muusiko music
musmaar nail
musmaar maraara leh screw
musqul bathroom; toilet
mustacmarad colony; protectorate
muufee bake
muxibbo admiration

N

-na and
nabad peace
nabad gelyo peace; safe; goodbye!
nabaad guur erosion
nabad ilaalin peace-keeping
nabad sugid security
nabar scar
nacas stupid person
nacbaysi unpleasantness
nacnac sweet
nadh *metal* nut
nadiif(i) clean
naadir rare
nafaqo nutrition

nafaqo xumo malnutrition
naflay living organism
naftihawir adventure
naag woman
nagaadi settlement
nagdayn tanning
najaar carpenter
nal light
nambar number
naqdi cash
naqil copy
naqshad drawing; model; pattern
nasasho rest
nasiib fortune; luck
nasiibdarro bad luck
naastaro record player; tape recorder
naxariis kindness
naxariis la'aan unkindness
naxariislaawe barbaric
nayl lamb
nayloon nylon
neecow dhuleed breeze
neef gas
neef ceerin natural gas
neef engegan dry gas
neefi to blow
neefqaadasho inspiration
neefso to breathe
neefsasho oksajiin la' anaerobic respiration
neefsasho oksajiin leh aerobic respiration
neefsasho respiration; breathing
nibiri whale
nidaamsan neat
niman men
nin man; husband
niyad moral
noobiyad lighthouse
Noofembar November
noog tired
nool alive; living
nool ku to live in
nolol dag biosphere
nololraacdaysi livelihood
noqo: ku soo noqo return to
noqod reflection

nud tissue
nuuge suction pump
nuugis absorption
nuxur subsistence; nourishment
nuxurleh nourishing

O

oo and
oday old man; elder
oogada dhulka lithosphere
oggolow to allow; to approve; to ratify
oohi to cry
oktoobar October
olol flame
orod run
-ow *masculine vocative suffix*

Q

qaab shape
qaab darane irregular
qaabka dhulka land forms
qab dhaaf proud
qabatin adaptation
qabo to catch; to hold; **soo qabo** to reach
qaboojiiye cool; refrigerator
qabow cold
qabow dhaaf to freeze
qabsasho invasion
qabso take hold
qadaadiic penny
qaad take
qaaddo spoon
qaadi judge
qaadid lift
qadar destiny
qadee to have lunch
qadh-qadhyo shiver
qadhaabasho food gathering
qadhaadh bitter
qadhabi buckle

qado dinner; lunch
qaado to get; to take
qafas cage
qalaad isjiidad adhesion
qalaad stranger
qalaad extensive
qalab ciyaareed top
qalab equipment; instrument; tool
qalab waxsoosaar *means of production*
qalabka muusiga instrument
qalabka tacabka *means of production*
qalabka wax lagu kariyo cooker
qalcad castle; fort
qalalaase disturbance
qalayl dry
qalayn discrimination
qaleyl dried
qaali something expensive
qalin khad pen
qalin pen
qalin qori; qalin rasaas ah pencil
qallooc curve
qalloocan refraction; bent; curved
qalqallooc meander; zigzag
qaamuus dictionary
qandac warm
qandi bag; handbag
qaniin to bite; to sting
qaniinyo bite
qanjaafilo hooves
qanjaafulay ungulates
qanjaruufo pinch
qanjidh dheefshiid digestive gland
qanjidh dhidid sweat gland
qanjiidho to pinch
qanjo barar mumps
qaan gaar mature
qaanso rainbow
qarannimo sovereignty
qarax eruption
qardaas card; cardboard
qariib stranger
qarni century
qarrar faulting

qarxiye fuse
qas mix; mess
qasab sugar cane; straw
qasabad tap
qasacad can; tin
qashin garbage; litter; rubbish
qashinsaar excretion
qaxwe coffee
qayb part; share
qaybin distribution
qaybsan divided
qaybsasho share
qaylo noise; shout
qaaayo valuable; price; quality
qeexid definition
qiimee evaluate
qiimo valuable; price; quality
qiimo dhin depreciation
qiimo leh valuable
qiiq sii daaye chimney
qiiq smoke
qiire-qiire critical
qiro admit
qiyaam values
qiyaas dhuleed acre
qiyaas scale; average
qiyaasi weigh
qod dig
qodaal plantation
qodaal dhafan mixed farming
qodaal guur shifting cultivation
qodax thorn
qodobbo factors
qof person
qol room
qol dhusin cellar
qol hurdo bedroom
qolka cuntada dining room
qolka cuntada lagu kariyo kitchen
qolka fadhiga sitting room
qolka qubaysiga; qolka qubeyska bathroom
qolo race
qolof shell
qooley pigeon
qooqab crab
qoor neck
qoosh mix

qor to write
qorrax sun
qorrax dhac sunset
qorrax soo bax dawn; sunrise
qorfe cinnamon
qori wood; gun
qori dheecaan sap
qori goyn lumber work
qor to write
qorraato lizard
qorshe program
qosol laugh
qotin electrode
qotin tabane cathode
qoto dheer deep
qoton vertical
qoxooti refugee
qoyan wet
qoys family
qudaar vegetables
qudhaanjo ant
quudhid sacrifice
qudhmis decay
quduuc mean
quful lock
qulaanqulshe larynx
qulqul current
qumbe coconut
quraac breakfast
quraaco to have breakfast
Quraan Qur'an
quraar sculpture
quraarad bottle; glass
qurbin fragmentation
quruurux pebble; gravel
qurux beautiful; beauty
qurux badan beautiful
quruxsan beautiful
qurxi decorate
quwad strong

R

rab to want; to wish
Rabbi God
rabitaan willing

rablo plait
raac to accompany; **gaadhi raac** to go by car
raad effect
raadi seek
raadyatoore radiator
raf shelf
rag men
ragcad prostration in prayer
rah frog
rajee hope
rajistar register
rajo wish
raajo x-ray
rakaab passenger
rakaad frequency
raalli ahow! excuse me!
raqiis cheap
rar la'aan unload
raas family; to accompany
raasamaal capital
raasamaal wareega circulating capital
rasaas bullet; ammunition
rasaas joojin ceasefire
raashin provisions
rash qarxin firework
raasi peninsula
rasiidh receipt
raydiiyow radio
ra'yi idea
raaxo la'aan uncomfortable
reer (extended) family; group of related people
reer guuraa nomads
reer magaal townspeople
rhoodhi duban toast
ri nanny goat
rib contraction
ribnaan concentration
rid drop
ridiq to mince
rikoodh record
rikoor tape recorder
rinji paint
rinjiga dhar dye
riwaayad play
riix push

riixo press
riyo goats
roob rain; rainfall
roob beeg rain gauge
roobka sannadka annual rainfall
roodhi bread
roog carpet
rooti bread
rooxaan mystical
rubuc quarter
rumaysi believe
rumaysi realize
run reality; truth
runtii of course!
ruqur bud
ruqurayn budding
ruqur dhadhan taste bud
ruqur surdhubeed axillary bud
ruqur ubax flowering plant
ruxrux shake

S/SH

saab calyx
sabab reason
saabaan apparatus
sabiib (madow) currants; raisins
sabiib sultana
saabka jidhka skeleton
sabo habitat
saabsan ku concerning
sabti saturday
saabuun soap
sabuurad blackboard
sac cow
saacad hour; watch; time
saacad wareeg clockwise
saacad weyn clock
sacaaf plankton
saadaasha hawada weather forecast
saddex three
saf line; queue
safaana savanna
safar journey; voyage; travel
safaysan refined

safee clean
saafi plain
safiir ambassador
sagaal nine
sagaashan ninety
sagxad badda ocean floor
sahame explorer
sahlan easy
sakaar sternum
sakiin razor
sal base
sal carays continental shelf
salaad prayer
salaan ladder; stairs; to greet
salaasa Tuesday
salbuko pea
saldhig station
saldhig milatari military base
saldhigga saadka supply base
saliid oil
saliloos cellulose
salli prayer mat
samay stalk
sambab lung
samee to do; to make; to fix; to manufacture
saami share
samo sky
san nose
saan hide
sanad year
saanad ammunition
sanbab lung
sanboor hay fever
sandal slipper
sandulayn imposition
sanduuq box
sanduuq-waraaqeed mailbox
saani straight
sannad sid dhaaf ah leap year
sanqad sound
sansaan form
sanuunad gravy
saqaf roof; ceiling; comb
saaqid induction
saar put on top of
saaran on top of
sare top; upper

sareeya high
sarif exchange
sarifo to exchange money
sariir bed
sariir carruureed cot; cradle
sarreen wheat
sawir photograph; picture; to draw
sawir jini-jini cartoon; cartoon
sawir qosol comic
sax correct; right
soo fadhiiso to sit down
soo jeed to stay awake
soo nabadgelyee to say goodbye
soo gado to buy
soo mar to pass along
soo dhowee welcome
soo dhowow to come in
soo deg to land
saxan basin; dish; plate
saaxiib *male* friend
saaxiibad *female* friend
saxir magic
saxni plate
saxaro feces
saynis yaqaan scientist
saynis science
sayruukh rocket
-se but
sebtember September
seeb paddle
seed ligament
seef sword
seeg miss
seesar saucer
seexasho sleeping
seexo sleep
shaabuug whip
shaac twilight
shaadh(i) shirt
shaag wheel; tire
shaah tea
shaandho sieve; strainer
shacaabi reef
shalay; shaleyto yesterday
shamac candle
shan five

shandad bag; handbag; suitcase
shaneemo film
shanlo comb
shaqal vowel
shaqaale worker; laborer
shaqaale cunteed a cook
shaqaale guur-guura migrant labor
shaqee to work
shaqo work; labor; job; profession
shaqo jujuub ah; shaqo ku qasab forced labor
shaqo-raadin dibedeed migrant labour
sharabaad sock
sharabaad xuub stocking
sharxi to decorate
sharci law
shamaca xaydhiisa wax
shaxan art; figures
shay substance
shaybaar laboratory
shebeg net
sheeg tell
sheeko baralay myth
sheeko story
sheekooyin beryo hore ah myth
shay material
shiid to mince
shidaal fuel
shidan lit
shil accident
shiil to fry
shiilan fried
shimbir bird (not a bird of prey)
shiine china
shineemo film
shinni bee
shinyeeriga zip
shiiqiye dominant
shir meeting; assembly
shiish target; aim
shishe far
shisheeye foreign
shii-shiid puree
shokad fork
shub to pour
shucaabi corals
shufti bandit

shukumaaso towel
shuuliyo bracelet
shummi kiss
shuruudo criteria
si way
sii away; to give; to pay; to supply
siib zip
sibiibix smooth
sibiibixo slide
sibiil furubo stigma
sicir price
sida caadiga ah usually
sidaas darteed because of that; therefore
sidde handle
siddeed eight
siddeetan eighty
sidee how
sii deyn lose
sigaar cab smoke
sii iibso to sell
siiye guud universal donor
silbo slip
silig wire
silsilad chain; necklace
silsilad cunto food chain
sir secret
siraad lamp
sisin sesame
sii wad to continue
sixir magic
sixni dish
sixniga-qubaysiga bath
siyaado abundance
siyaasad politics
soo towards here
soo bax to rise up
soco to go; to continue; to accompany
socod motion
socoto travelers
soddon thirty
soohdin boundary; frontier
soke near
sonkor sugar
soofe sofa; file (tool)
Soomaali Somali person
soor porridge

soore host
soosaarayaal producers
soosaarid production
su'aal question
subag butter
suubaan alluvium
subax morning
subitoor whip
sudh hang
suuf wool; cotton wool
sug wait
sugan absolute
suugaan literature
suugo sauce
sukiini courgette
suul thumb
suldaantooyo sultanate
suuli lavatory
sulub steel
summad name; mark; symbol
sun poison
suun belt
suune eyebrow
suuq market
suuq madow black market; informal economy
suuq-sooran (side EU) Common Market
surwaal trousers
surwaal gaaban short trousers
suuxid unconsciousness
suxul elbow
suxuun plates

T

tab technique
tabaashiir chalk
taabasho touch
tababbar training
tacab production
tacliin education
tag go; leave
taag hill
taagan ka facing
taageero support

tagsi taxi
tagsile taxi driver
tahar tendon
taaj crown
taajir trader
takfi flea
takoor segregate
taksi taxi
talaagad refrigerator
tali u dictate
talifishan television
tallaabo step
talo advice; decision
talo geli to seek advice (**ka** from)
talogelyo seeking advice
tallaal vaccine; vaccination
tamaandho tomato
tamar energy
tanbuug camp
taandho tent
tantoon fist
taraq match
tarrijis extension
tartan race
taloggal consider
tax-dhaxaltooyo dynasty
taxa maamulka bureaucracy
taayir wheel
tayo quality
tayroodh thyroid
teknooloji technology
telefishan television
telefoon; telifoon telephone
telefoon dir telephone (**u** someone)
teendho camp
termuus thermos flask
tidic plait
tif taf capillary
tigidh stamp; ticket
tijaabo experiment
tilmaan to describe
timir dates
timo hair
timo aan run ahayn wig
tin hair
tiin cactus
tiir pillar
tiirada dadka population

tiirada qaaradeed continental slope
tiiraanyo depression
tirayn railway
tiri to count
tiriig lamp
tiro number; quantity
tiiro slope; gradient
tiro koobka dadka population
  census
tiirso lean
tirsan counted
tirtir to rub; to wipe
tixraac refer
toob robe
toban ten
toobin cone
toddoba seven
toddobaad week
toddobaatan seventy
tog ravine; dry valley
toogo shoot
tol to sew; to mend
tolan stitch; suture
toliin sewing
toon garlic
toorri dagger
toos directness; straightness; direct;
  to wake; to get up; to stand up;
  to be straight
toosan straight; upright
toosi wake someone up
toxob dandruff
tub orbit
tuubo siphon
tufaax apple
tuug burglar; thief
tukasho prayer
tuko pray
tuulo village
tuman ground
tun to hit; to grind
tuur to throw
turjumida interpretation
tus show
tusid show
tusmada girid grid reference
tusmo khariidadeed reference
tuwaal towel

U

ubax flower
ubo-ubax pistil
ubuc abdomen
u eegid relative
ugaadhsi hunting
ugax side yar ovule
ugax egg
ugbaad fresh grass
ugedi convert
ugxan egg
ugxanside ovary
ujeeddo aim
ujeeddo purpose
ukun eggs (chicken)
ul stick
ul tin hair shaft
uumi bax evaporation
uumi biyood water vapour
uumibax evaporation
uumihoorow condensation
uun universal
unug cell
uur pregnant
ur smell
urur assembly
uurjiif embryo
uur leh pregnant
urur shaqaale trade union
uskag dirty

W

waa epoch; to fail; to miss
waabbay venom
waabeeri dawn
wacan: ugu wacan best
wacatan to make a pact
wacdi to preach
wad to continue; to drive
wada together
wadahadal talks
wadajir together
waddan land; country; nation

waddo lane; road
wadne heart
wadneed cardiac
wado xadiid railroad
waddo to drive a car
waddo-cageed pavement
waa hagaag! ok!
wahsi inertia
waajibaad duties
waa kan . . . here is . . .
wakhtigii while
wakiil representative
waal to make mad
walaal brother; sister
walaaq mix
walaaq isku stir up
walaal sister
walba each; every
walhade pendulum
waalid parent
waliinjo box
wallaah really!
waalo to go mad
wanaagsan good; nice; well
wan ram
waani to recommend
Waaq God
waqooyi north
waqti time
waqti dhaw recent
waqti fiican fun
war lake; news
waraabe hyena
waraabin irrigation
waraaq paper
waraaqo qoraal mail
waran spear
wardoon intelligence *(spying)*
waare permanent
wareeg revolution; rotation; to go around; to revolve; to tour
wareegsan round
wareegsan ku surrounded by
wareysi interview
wargeys magazine
war ileed oasis
warqad letter; paper
warqad gaaban note

warran to give news (**ka** about)
warshad factory
warshadeyn industrialisation
warshed industry
war-side newspaper
waryaa hey!; hi!
wasaaqyo earring
wasdaad builder
wasiir minister
wasiirka arrimaha dibadda foreign minister
wax thing
waxba nothing
waxbarasho learning
waxsoosaar production; output
waxtar leh useful
waxtar usefulness
wayne major
waayo because; why?
webi river
weji face
wejiga dayaxa lunar phase
weel deposit
weli still; yet
welwel worry
weerar attack
weerar qaad attack
weydii to ask
weyn big
weyneyn magnification
wiil boy
wiqiyad ounce
wiriq crystal
wiish elevator
wisikh dirty
wiyil rhinoceros

X

xab amniotic fluid
xabag glue; to stick
xabaal grave
xabbad bullet; piece; unit
xabsi prison
xabuub grain(s)
xad boundary; limit

xadhig string; rope; line
xadhiga kabaha lace
xadhko chords
xadidan limited
xadiid iron; steel
xadiid ciideed cast iron
xadiidka railway
xadiidlab steel
xaafad quarter
xafid preserve
xaflad party; reception
xag direction; side
xagaa dry season (July to August)
xagaashin southwest trade wind
xagal angle
xagal gooye diagonal
xaggee where
xagli to favour; to tend
xaglin bias
xaakimada iyo maxkamadaha
    judiciary
xaakin judge
xalleefsan flat
xallin settlement
xaamilo pregnant
xammaal porter
xamaam bathroom
xamayti bile
xammuul load
xanaaq anger; heat
xannaanadda digaaga poultry
xanshasheq whisper
xanuun ache; pain
xaq just
xaaq to sweep; to exterminate
xaqi jurisdiction
xaqiiji to confirm; to prove
xaaqin broom
xaqiiq truth
xaqiiq ah actual
xaar feces
xaraf letter
xarafaha alphabet
xareed rain water
xareedeyn distillation
xarfiye condenser
xariifnimo intelligence
xariiqa taariikh sooca international

date line
xariiqa xeebta coast line
xariir silk
xariif clever
xarun capital; institution
xaas wife; wife & children; family
xaashi paper
xasuus recollect
xataa even
xatabad step
xawaare speed
xawaash spices
xaaxeeyo snail
xayawaan animals
xayawaan guri joog ah pet
xayeesi lean
xayir block
xeeb beach; coast
xeebta badda bay; beach
xeedho dish
xeer law
xeer-beyti fury
xeydaan fence
xiddig star
xiddigis astronomy
xidh to fasten; to tie; to shut; to
    close
xidhan closed; to be closed;
    dressed; to be tied
xidhe lock
xidhiidh relation
xidid root; vein
xidid maskaxeed medulla
xiiran shave
xiiso interest
xiiso leh interesting
xil responsibility
xilli season
xiribo eyelids
xisaab account
xisbi political party
xishood shy
xoghaye secretary
xoog strong; force; army
xoogahaan violent
xoogsato proletariat
xool cot
xoolaley livestock keepers

xoolo

xoolo domestic livestock
xoolo dhaqato pastoral
xordan luqumeed cervix
xornimo freedom
xuub membrane
xubin member; segment
xuddun umbilical cord
xuddun cufisjiidad centre of gravity
xuddun fur decentralised
xuduud frontier
xufrad pit
xukumad government
xukun dadban indirect rule
xulasho selection
xulufo allies
xummad sheeg thermometer

xun bad; nasty
xunbo foam

Y

yaab leh marvelous
yaab to be surprised
yaanyo tomato
yar little; small
yaraan: ugu yaraan minimum
yariis tiny
yeedh u to call someone
yeelo to have; to hold
yey wild dog
yuuriya urea

ENGLISH-SOMALI
INGRIISI-SOMAALI

A

abdomen ubuc
ability karti
able: to be able kar
abroad dal qalaad
absent maqan
absolute sugan
absorption fuuqis
abundance siyaado
abuse af-lagaado
accent lahjad
accept aqbal
accident shil
accommodate hoysii
accompany la soco
account xisaab
accurate hufan
accuse dacwee
acid aasiidh
acquaintance macrufo
acre qiyaas dhuleed
acrobat ciyaaryahan xirfad leh
act samee
activity dhaqdhaqaaq
actuality run
ache xanuun
adaptation qabatin
add isku dar
add to ku dar
address cinwaan
adhesion qalaad isjiidad
adhesive xabag
admit qir
adventure naftihawir
advice talo
advisory council golaha la
  taliyayaasha
aerobic respiration neefsasho
  oksajiin leh
aeroplane dayuurad
fear baqdin
Africa Afrika

after ka dib
afternoon galab
afterwards ka dib
age group iskufac
age da'
aggregate cuntub
agnostic cawaan
agreement heshiis
ah! hayye
Aids Aydis
aim shiish
air bladder hawo hays
air sacs kiish haweed
air hawo
airport garoon dayuuradeed
alimentary canal cunto mareen
alive nool
alkaline alkalayn
alone keli
alphabet xarafaha
aluminum jaandi
allergy cadanyo
alliance isbahaysi; **to make an
  alliance** isbahayso
allies xulufo
allow oggolow
alluvium suubaan
amalgamation midayn
ambassador safiir
ambulance ambalaas
ammunition rasaas
amniotic fluid xab
amount in
anchor baroosin
and iyo
anerobic respiration neefsasho
  oksajiin la'
angel malaa'ig
anger cadho
angle xagal
angry cadhosan; **to get angry**
  cadhow
animal xayawaan; **wild animals**
  habardugaag

ankle canqow
announce baaq; dhawaaq
annual rainfall roobka sannadka
answer jawaab
ant qudhaanjo
antagonism isnac
antenna gees dareen
anther faxaliid
anti lid
anti-clockwise lidsaacad wareeg
antibiotic antibaayootik
antibody lid-jidh gale
antigen lid-gal
antitoxin lid mariid
aorta gar
apartheid midabtakoor
ape daanyeer
apparatus saabaan
apple tufaax
approve oggolow
April Abriil
arab carab
area bed; gobol
arm gacan
armchair kursi
army askar
arrive gaadh
arrow falaadh
art shaxan; fan
arteriole halbawle yare
artesian well ceelka aartiis
artist farshaxan
ask weydii
asleep: to be asleep seexo
assembly shir
assimilation beelaysi
atheist diinlaawe
atmosphere atmoosfeer
atom aton
attack *noun* weerar
attack *verb* weerar qaad
attitude dabci
attraction jiidasho
aubergine bidingal
audibility maqalkarid
audience daawaadayaal
august agoosto
aunt *paternal* eedo
aunt *maternal* habaryar
authority awood
autumn dayr

average qiyaas
awake kicid
away sii
ax gudin
axillary bud ruqur surdhubeed
axis dhidib

B

baby cunug
bacillus bausilas
back part dabo
bacteria bakteeriye
bad xun
bag shandad; boorso
bag *plastic carrier* bac
bake dub
baker dube
balance miisaan
bald bidaar
ball kubbad
balloon buufin
banana muus
bandit budhcad
bank bangi
barbaric cawaan
barometer cadaadis beeg
barrel barmiil; foosto
barrier carqalad
base sal
basin saxan
basket danbiil
bat *animal* fidmeer
bat *wooden* loox
bath sixniga-qubaysiga
bathroom qolka qubeyska
battle dagaal
bay gacan
be in a place jir
beach xeebta badda
bead(s) kuul
beak afka shimbiraha
bean(s) digir
beard gadh gar
beautiful quruxsan
beauty qurux
because of that sidaas darteed
because waayo; maxa yeelay
bed sariir

bedcover kuberto
bedroom qol hurdo
bee shinni
beetle cayayaan
begin bilaab
behavior dabci
behind dambe
believe rumaysi
belonging to ka tirsan
belt suun
bell koor
belly buruc
bent qalloocan
berry midho yar
between dhexe
bias kalajeclaysi
bicycle baaskeelad; bushkuleeti
big weyn
bile xamayti
biosphere nolol dag
bird shimbir
bird of prey haad
birthday maalintaad dhalatay
biscuit buskut
bite qaniin
bitter qadhaadh
black madow
black market suuq madow
blackboard sabuurad
bladder kaadihays
blanket buste
block xayir
blockade cunaqabatayn
blow neefi
blue buluug
board loox
boat dooni
body jidh; jidhka
boil *verb* kar; kari
boil *noun* kasoobbax
boiling karaya
bolt bool
bone laf
book buug
boot buudh; kab
borrow amaah
bottle dhalo
bottom hoos
boundary xad
bowl madiibad
box waliinjo

boxer feedhyahan
boy inan; wiil
bracelet shuuliyo
bran buushe
branch laan
brave geesi
bread kimis; rooti; kibi; roodhi
breadth ballaadh
break jabi
breakfast quraac; **to have
    breakfast** quraaco
breath neefsasho
tired noog
breeze neecow dhuleed
brick leben
bridge buundo
bright iftiin
bring keen
broad ballaadhan
broadness ballaadh
broken jaban
broom xaaqin
brother aboowe; walaal
brown boodhe
brush burush/buraash
bucket baaldi
buckle qadhabi
bud ruqur
Buddhism diinta buudaha
budding ruqurayn
bug cayayaan
build dhis
builder wasdaad
building daar
building *activity* dhisid
bulb *electric* guluub
bullet rasaas; xabbad
bureaucracy taxa maamulka
burglar tuug
burn gubo
burn *something* gub
burnt guban
bus gaadiidka weyn; bas
bush geed-cuf
busy *active* hawlan; *occupied*
    mashquul
but -se; laakiin
butcher hilibleh
butter burcad
butter badhar; subag
butterfly balanbaalis

button badhan
buy gado; iibso
by agteeda

C

cabbage kaabash
cactus tiin
cage qafas
cake keeg
calamity masiibo
calculator kalkulatar
calico mareykaan
calorie kaaloori
call *someone* u yeedh; **I am called**
 ... Magacaygu waa ...
callus gaatir
camel awr; *female* hal
camels geel
camera kamarad
camp tanbuug
can qasacad
canal kelli
candle shamac
cannon bunduq-madfac
canoe dooni yar
cap koofiyad
capacity mug
capillary tif taf
capital *financial* hanti
capital city magaalomadax
capitalist hanti-goosi
car baabuur; fatoorad; gaadhi
card qardaas
cardamom heyl
cardboard qardaas
cardiac wadneed
carnivorous hilib cune
carpenter najaar
carpet roog
carrot kaaradh
cart gaadhi faras
cartilage carjow
cartoon sawir qosol
cash naqdi
cash crop dalag ganac
cassava moxoggo
cassette tape cajalad
castle qalcad

cat bisad
catch qabo
caterpillar dirindiir
cathedral kinisad weyn
cathode qotin tabane
cattle lo'
cause dhali
cave god
ceasefire rasaas joojin
ceiling saqaf
cell structure dhisme-unug
cell unug
cellar qol dhusin
center badhtarne
center of town farasmagaalo
century qarni
cereal firiley
cervix xordan luqumeed
cinnamon qorfe
circle goobaabin
circus carwo dad
city centre farasmagaalo
city magaalo
civil war dagaal sokeeye
clan qabiil
clarify caddee
class *social* dabaqad
class *school* dir
classification kal a-soocid
classification abla-ablayn
classroom fasal
clay dhoobo
clean safee
clear: to make clear caddee
clever xariif
climate cimilo
climb kor u kor
clock saacad (weyn)
clockwise saacad wareeg
close xidh
closed xidhan
cloth dhar; maro
clothes dharka
clothing *women's* mar
cloud(s) daruur
clove dhegayare
clown majaajileeye
co-operative iskaadhato
coast xeeb
coast line xariiqa xeebta
coat jaako

cobbler kabo tolle
coconut qumbe
coffee qaxwe
coin beesad
cold *noun* dhaxan
cold *adjective* qabow
cold *illness* duray
colony mustacmarad
color midab
collar kaladh
collective beer kooxeed
comb shanlo
come after dambee
come in soo dhowow
come in! dhowow: soo dhowow!
comic sawir qosol
commercial ganacsi
committee gole
common market suuq-sooran (side EU)
commonwealth barwaaqo-sooran
community mujtamac
compass jiheeye
composite isku dhisan
compression diisnaan
comprised of ka kooban
computer kambiyuutar
concentration ribnaan
concerning ku saabsan
condensation uumihoorow
condenser xarfiye
conduction gudbin
cone toobin
confirm xaqiiji
conflict: to be in conflict with ka soo horjeed
confluence iskudar
confrontation iska horimaad
conservation kaydin
consider taloggal
construction dhismo
continue u soco; sii wad
contour joog ekeeye
contraception ka hor-taga uur qaadidda
contraction rib
contradiction isburin
convection islabarog
conventional sign calaamadaha la doortay
convert ugedi

cook kari
cook *person* shaqaale cunteed
cook *verb* kari
cooked: to be cooked bislow
cooker qalabka wax lagu kariyo
cooking bislayn
cooking pot maddiibad
cool qabow
copper maar
copy *noun* naqil
copy *verb* guuris
corals shucaabi
cork quf
correct sax
cot sariir carruureed
cot xool
cottage guri cariish
cotton cudbi
cotton cloth bafto
cotton wool suuf
couch kursi dheer
count tiri
counted tirsan
counter miis dukaan
country dhul
countryside baadiye
courgette sukiini
course: of course! runtii
court maxkamad
cousin ina-adeer
cover dabool
cow sac
crab qooqab; carsaanyo
cradle sariir carruureed
craft farsamad, farshaxan
crash program barnaamijka (cuntada) degdegga
criteria shuruudo
critical qiire-qiire
crop rotation dalag gedis
crops dalag
cross section jeebis gudub
cross *noun* gudbid
cross *verb* gudub
cross-pollination faxal gudbin-tallaabin
crown kug
crumb burbur roodhiyeed
cry *shout* ilmo; *weep* oohi
crystal wiriq

cucumber khajaar; khiyaar
cultivate beer
cup koob
cupboard armaajo
currants sabiib
current *water* madhxiye; *electric* koronto
curtain(s) daah
curve qallooc
curved qalloocan
cushion barkin
cut go'
cuticle toxob
cutlery alaabta wax lagu cuno
cyclonic rain gufaacaale
cylinder dhululubo
chain silsilad
chair kursi
chalk jeeso
change beddel
characteristics astaamo
charcoal dhuxul
charge *electric* danabayn
chase eryo
cheap jaban
cheat khiyaamo
check jeeg garee
cheek dhaban
cheese foormaajo
chicken digaag; dooro
child ilmo yar; cunug; ilmo
children carruur
chilli pepper basbaas
chimney qiiq sii daaye
chin gadh; gar
china shiine
chisel jiisel
chlorophyl cagaariye
chocolate jokolaato
chop up jarjar
chords xadhko
christian kristaan
christmas iida kristamasaka
chromosomes koromesoomis
chrysalis karaysalis
church kiniisad

D

dagger toori
dairy caano diiq
dance *noun* ciyaar
dance *verb* dheel
danger khatar
dangerous khatar
dark madow
darkness mugdi
date palm geedka timirta
dates timir
daughter gabadh; inan
dawn waabeeri
day beri; casho; maalin
daylight ilays dharaareed
D.D.T. di-di-ti
death dhimasho
debris miiqlay
decay qudhmis
December Disembar
decentralised baahin
decision go'aan
declare caddee
decorate sharxi
deep qoto dheer
defects iimo
defense difaac
definition qeexid
deflection baydhis
degree digrii
delay u kaadi
den god bahal
density cufnaan
dental ilkood
dentist dhakhtarka ilkaha
deposit weel
depreciation qiimo dhin
depression *land* bohol; *medical* tiiraanyo; *economic* ceriiri dhaqaale
describe tilmaan
desert lamadegaan
desire rab
desk miis
destiny aayatiin
destroy bi'i
destroyed: to be destroyed ba'
determination go'aansasho

development horumar
deviation leexad
dew dharab
diagonal xagal gooye
dial *verb* garaac
diameter dhex roor
diamond dheemman
diary buug xasuus qor
dictate u tall
dictator keligii-taliye
dictionary qaamuus
die dhimo
diet cunto
different kala duwan
differentiation kala-saarid
difficult adag
difficulty dhib
diffusion baahid
dig faag
digestion dheefshiid
digestive gland qanjidh dheefshiid
digits faro
dilute badhax
dine cashee
dining room qolka cuntada
dinner casho
dinner: to have dinner cashee
direct current danab qumman
direct toos
direction xag
directness toos
dirty uskag; wisikh
disappear libidh
discriminate kala sooc
discrimination qalayn
discussion hadal
dish xeedho
disk daawe
dispersal firdhis
disperse firdhi
displaced person qaxooti
displacement barabbaxin
distance fogaansho
distillation xareedeyn
distribution qaybin
disturbance qalalaase
diverging firdhiso
diversification (of crops) kala
   duwid
divided qaybsan
divorce fur

do samee
doctor *male* dhakhtar; *female*
   dhakhtarad
dog ey
dollar doollar
dominant shiiqiye
donkey dameer
donor deeqe
door irrid
double labanlaab
d.p. *see* displaced person
drainage system habka biyo shubka
draw sawir
drawing naqshad
dress *woman's* guntiino; *clothes*
   labisasho
dressed xidhan
dried qaleyl
drink cab
drink milk dhan (dhamaa)
drip dhibic
drive animals kexee
drive a car wado
drop dhac
drought abaar
drum durbaan
dry *verb* engeji
dry *adjective* qalayl
dry season (December to March)
   jiilaal
dry season (July to August) xagaa
dry valley tog
dualism labaale
duck boolo-boolo
dust boor; boodh
duties waajibaad
dye *noun* rinjiga dhar
dye *verb* midabee
dynasty tax-dhaxaltooyo

E

each kasta
ear dheg
early goor hore
earring wasaaqyo
earth *ground* dhul; *planet* meere
earthquake dhul gariir
east bari

easy fudud
eat cun
eclipse madoobaad
ecology ikooloji
economic depression hoos-u-dhac dhaqaale
economic stagnation dhaqaale fadhiid ah
economic struggle cunoqabatayn dhaqaale
economy dhaqaale
ecosystem habdhis ikooloji
echo dayaan
edge geftin
education barasho
effect raad
efficiency karti
egg ugxan
eggplant bidingal
eggs *chicken* ukun
egoism anaaniyad
eight siddeed
eighty siddeetan
elasticity laastiko
elbow suxul
elder *person* oday
electric koronto ah
electrification danabayn
electrode qotin
electromagnetism birlabdanabow
electron elektaron
electroscope danabtuse
electrostatic danad beg
elephant maroodi
elevator wiish
embryo uurjiif
emission bixin
emit bixi
empire imbaraaduuriyad
empty madhan
enamel dheeh
end *noun* dhammaad
end *verb* gebogebbee
endocardium gudowadneed
endurance adkaysi
enemy cadow
energy tamar
engine makiinad
enjoy hel ka
enter gal
entertain *guests* martiqaad

envelope gal waraaqeed
environment deegaan
enzyme ensayn
epidermis dub sare
epiglottis cidhib
epoch waa
equator badhe
equilibrium dheelitiran
equipment qalab
erosion nabaad guur
eruption qarax
escape baxso
escarpment duud
especially khaas ahaan
European Union Midowga Yurub
evacuate daadguree
evaluate qiimee
evaporation uumibax
even xataa
evening habeen; **to spend the evening** cawee; **this evening** caawa
every kasta
examine day
exchange isdhaafsi; sarif
exchange money sarifo
exciting farxad leh
excretion qashinsaar
excuse me! raalli ahow!
exfoliation falfalliiran
existence jiritaan
expand fidi
expansion fidis
expectation filitaan
expensive *thing* qaali
experiment tijaabo
explain caddee
exploitation ka faa'iidaysi
explorer sahame
export dhoofi
extension fidin
extensive qalaad
exterior debed
exterminate xaaq
external dabadeed
extra dheeraad ah
extract bixi
eye il
eyeball gumuca isha
eyebrow suune
eyelids xiribo

F

fabric dhar
face weji
facial nerve dareenside waji
facing ka taagan
factors qodobbo
factory warshad
fail waa
fair carwo
fall dhac
fall *rain* da'
fallopian tube dhuunta faloob
fame caan
family bah; qoys; *extended* reer
fan babis
fan marawaxad
far (from) fog (ka)
farm beer
farmer beeroley
farming, commercial beeris ganaceed
fascinating xiiso leh
fascination xiiso
fascist fishiisto
fast dhakhso
fasten xidh
fat *noun* baruur
fat *adjective* buuran
father aabbe
favour xagli
feather baal
features muuqaal
February Febraayo
feces saxro
feed cuntee
feet cago
femur bawdo
fence xeydaan
fertile soil carro-san
fertility bacrinnimo
fertilization bacrimin
fertilizer bacrimiye
fetch keen
fetus ilmo uur ku jira
feudal dhulgoosi
few dhowr
fibrous liilan

fibula biixi-yar
field dhul beereed garoon
fifty konton
fight dagaal
fighting dagaal
figures shaxan
file fayl; *tool* soofe
film *cinema* shineemo; *camera* filim
fill buuxi
find hel
finger far
finish dhammee
fire dab; gubasho
fire-engine dab demis
firewood xaabo
firework rash qarxin
first kowaad
first-born child curad
firstly marka hore
fish kalluun
fisherman kaluumayste
fist tantoom
five shan
fix hagaaji
flag calan
flame holac
flat balaadhan
flatworm gooryaan suun
flea booddo
flesh eater hilib cune
flood fatah
flood plain bannaan fatah
floor dabaq
flour budo
flower ubax
fluid dareere
fly *verb* duul
fly *noun* dukhsi
foam isbuunyo
focus kulmis
fog ceeryaamo; ceeryaan
fold buur duuban
folded laaban
follow dabo socod
food cunto
food chain silsilad cunto
food gathering cunto ururin

food processor

food processor mashiinka cuntada shiidan
fool nacas
foot cag
football kubadda cagta
force xoog
forced labor shaqo jujuub ah
forces *armed* ciidamo
forehead food
foreign shisheeye
foreign minister wasiirka arrimaha dibadda
forest hawd
fork foog/fargeeti
fork shokad
form sansaan
formal habsan
fort qalcad
fortune nasiib
forty afartan
forward gogoldhig
fossil foosil
fountain il-biyood
four afar
fox dawaco
fragmentation qurbin
freedom xornimo
freeze qabow dhaaf
frequency rakaad
fresh cusub
fresh grass ugbaad
friction isliska
Friday jimce
fried shiilan
friend *female* saaxiibad
friend *male* saaxiib
frightened: to be frightened baqo
frighten cabsi
frog rah
front part hor
frontier soohdin
frost dhedo
fruit midho; miro
fry shiil
fuel shidaal
slope tiiro
full dheregsan
full: to be full up dhereg
furniture alaabo guri
fun waqti fiican
fundamental aasaasi

fur dhogor
fury xeer-beyti
fuse badbaadiye

G

gap gaab
garage geerash
garbage qashin
garden beer
garlic toon
gas hawo; gaas
gate albaab
gene jiin, hiddoshid
general guud
generator dhaliye
genetics hiddo barasho
geology barashada dhulka
germination biqil; magool
get ka qaado
get up toos
giraffe geri
girl gabadh
give sii
glass *substance* muraayad; *drinking* dhalo
glove gacmo-gelis
glue xabag
go bax
go around wareeg
go by car gaadhi raac
go with raac
goal gool
goat: nanny goat ri
goats riyo
God Allaah
God willing! Haddii Eebbe yidhaahdo!
gold dahab
good wanaagsan
goodbye nabad gelyo; to say goodbye to soo nabadgelyee
goods badeeco
government dawlad; xukumad
gown *woman's* guntiino
gradient hoobad
grain xabuub
grandfather awoowe

grandmother abooto; ayeeyo
grapefruit bambeelmo
grapes canab
grass caws
grave xabaal
gravel quruurux
gravity cufisjiidad
gravy sanuunad
graze daaji
grazing land dhul-daaq
grease dufan
green doog
green vegetables dhimbiil
greet salaan
grid girid
grid reference tusmada girid
grill dub
grind tun
ground dhul
groundnut loos
group koox
grow koritaan
growth körid
guerrilla dagaal yahan jabhadeed
guess malee
guitar kaman
gulf gacan
gullies boholo
gun bunduq
gut galool yar

H

habit caado
habitat sabo
hair tin,
half badh
hammer burus; dubbe
hand gacan
handbag boorso
handkerchief masar
handle gacan
hang laalaad
happen dhac
happy farxad leh
happy: to be happy farax
harbor deked
hard adag
hardwood miici

hat koofiyad
have hay
hay caws qallalan
hay fever sanboor
head madax
health caafimaad
healthy ladan
hear maqal
hearing maqal
heart wadne
heat *noun* kuleyl
heat *verb* diiri
heated diiran
heavy culus
hectare hektaar
hedge dhir isku cufan
heel cidhib
height dherer
helicopter helikobtar
help *noun* caawimo
help *verb* u gargaar
hemaglobin hiimagoloobin
hemisphere galoob badh
hen digaag
herbalist geeda gooye
herbivorous daaq cune
herbs caleemo
here is . . . waa kan . . .
heredity hiddo
hermaphrodite labeeb
heterogeneous kalakaan
hey! heedheh!
hi! waryaa!
hibernation isxabaalid
hide dhuumasho
high korreeya
high latitude lool sare
high pressure cadaadis wayn
hill buur yar
hinduism diinta hindiga
hip misig
hippopotamus jeer
hit tun
hold hakin
hole god
holiday fasax
home hoy
honey malab
hoof qanjaaful
hook hangool
hookworm gooryaan jilaabeed

hoop giraangir
hope rajee
hormone hoormoon
horn gees
Horn of Africa Geeska Afrika
horse faras
hospital cusbataal
host soore
hot kulayl; *spicy* basbaas leh
hotel hudheel
hour saacad
house daar; *hut* minnan
housefly dukhsi
how sidee
human aadamiga
humanitarianism bani aadnimo
humerus cudud
humidity huur
humus hyuumas
hundred boqol
hunger gaajo
hungry gaajeysan
hunting ugaadhsi
hurry degdeg
hurt damqasho
husband nin
hut cariish
hybrid iska dhal
hydro-electric power awoodda danabka biyaha
hydrometer huur beeg
hydrosphere biyowlayda dhulka
hyena waraabe
hypothesis afeef

I

ice baraf
ice-cream jalaato
idea ra'yi
ideology idilooyiyad
letter xaraf
igneous rock dhadhaab shiileed
ill jirran
illumination if
imaginary la maleeyo
I.M.F. Hay'adda Lacagta Adduunka
immorality anshax xumo
impact radayn

imperialism imberiyaaliyad
import dibadda ka soo keen
imposition sandulayn
impulse gujo
incisors foolal
inclination janjeer
income dakhli
increase korodh; *(something)* kordhi
incubation period kal huuris
independence madax bannaanaan
independent madaxbannaan
Indian Ocean Badweynta Hindiga
indigenous dhalad
indirect rule gumaysi dahsoon
induction saaqid
industrial revolution kacaankii warshadaynta
industrialisation warshadeyn
industry warshed
inertia wahsi
infidel gaal
infiltration dhexgal; ku-qasan
informal economy suuq madow
ingestion cunto qaadasho
inheritance dhaxal
ink khad
inland drainage biyo shub oodan
input dalag
insect cayayaan
inside gudo
inspiration neef qaadasho
institution hab
instrument qalab
insulation magudbin
insulator mugudbiye
insurance caymis
intelligence caqli; *spying* basaasnimo
intensity itaal
interest dan
interesting xiiso leh
interference labid
interior gudo; *of country* miyi
internal combustion engine makiinad qubasho gudeed
international date line xariiqa taariikh sooca
international community adduunweyne
interpretation turjumid

interval biririf
intervene faraggeli
intervention faraggelin
interview wareysi
intestine mindhicir
invade dal qabso
invasion gelid
invest gelin
investigation baadhis
investment maal gelin
iris bu'
iron *metal* bir; feero; *cast* xadiid ciideed; *clothes* kaawiyad
ironing board miiska kaawiyadda
irregular qaab darane
irrigation waraabin
island jasiirad
isotherm heerkul madoorshe; kul-ekeeye
ivy dhilawyahan

J

jacket jaako
jam malmalaato
January janaayo
jaw daan
job shaqo
join isku xidhid
joint *noun* isgal
joint *adjective* laabato
joints kala goysyo
joke kaftan
joules juul
journal jariidad
journey safar
judge qaadi
judiciary xaakimada iyo maxkamadaha
jug ibriiq; jaag
July luulyo
jump bood
June juun
jungle aay jiq ah
jurisdiction xaqi
jury garsoorayaal
just *adjective* xaq ah

K

kettle jelemad
key fure
kick laad
kidney keli
kiln madbakh
kilogram kiilo; kiilograam
kill dil
kind naxariis leh
king boqor
kingdom boqortooyo
kiss dhunko
kitchen qolka cuntada lagu kariyo
kite abitey
kitten bisad yar
knee jilib
kneel jilbo joogsi
knife mindi
knob handaraab
knock garaac
knot guntin
know yiqiin
knowledge aqoon
Koran Quraan

L

labor shaqo
laboratory shaybaar
laborer shaqaale
lace xadhigga kabaha
ladder jaranjaro
lady marwo
lagoon haro baddeed
lake war
lamb nayl
lamp faynuus
land dhul; *fertile land* barwaaqo
land *aeroplane* soo deg
lane dhabo
language af
lap dhab
large weyn
large intestine midhicir weyne
larynx qulaan qulshe
last dambe

lateness daahid
latent period kalka qarsoon
latitude lool
laugh qosol
lava lafa
lavatory beetalmay
law sharci
lawn cagaar
lead hoggaamin
leader hoggaamiye
leaf caleen
lean xayeesi
leap kor u bood
leap year sannad sid dhaaf ah
learn baro
learning waxbarasho
leather harag
leather maas
leave bax
leeward dabayl ka jeed
left bidix
leg lug
lemon liin
lemonade liin miiran
length dherer
lens bikaac
leopard haramcad; shabeel
lesson cashar
letter warqad
lever kabaal
library laybreeri
lick leef
lid dabool
life cycle meerada nolosha
lift *noun* wiish
lift *verb* hinjin
ligament seed
light *noun* ilays
light *adjective* fudud
light *verb* nal
lighthouse noobiyad
lightning rod hillaac-danab tiir
like *presposition* sida
like *verb* ka hel
lime *fruit* liin
limestone didib
limit xad
limited xadidan
line saf
linen liinen
linguistic group koox afeed

lion libaax
lip dibin
lips dibno
liquid hoor
liquification hoorayn
list liis
listen dhegayso
lit shidan
literature suugaan
litter qashin
little yar
live nool
livelihood nololraacdaysi
liver beer
livestock keepers xoolaley
living organism naflay; noole
living nool
lizard qorraato
load xamuul
local time ammin meeleed
lock quful
log kurtin
long dheer
long rains (April to June) gu'
longitude dhige
longitudinal dhereran
look eeg
look at day
look for doondoon
lorry baabuur
loose debecsan
loud cod dheer
love jacayl
low hooseeya
low pressure cadaadis fudud yar
lower hoose
lower part hoos
luck nasiib
lunch qado; **to have lunch** qadee
lung sambab

M

macro ili-aragto
machine makiinad
mad: to go mad waalo; **to make mad** waal
magazine jariidad; wargeys
magic indhosarcaad

magnet birlab
magnetic birlaboobe
magnification weyneyn
magnitude laxaad
maid adeegto
mail waraaqo qoraal
mailbox sanduuq-waraaqeed
main muhiim
maize gallay
major *noun* gaashaanle
major *adjective* weyn
majority *political* aqlabiyad
make clear caddee
make garee
malaria duumo
malnutrition nafaqo xumo
malt ganaan
man nin
manager maamule
mandate awood-siin
mango cambe
manners dabeecad
manufactured samayn
manufacturing samayn
many badan
map khariidad
marble footari
March *month* maarso
march *verb* lugee
mark astaan
market bacadleh
married: to get married guurso
marrow dhuux
marry guursado
marshy land biyo fadhiisin
marvelous yaab leh
mask gedef
mass cuf
mat gogol; *prayer mat* masalle
match *football* tartan; *fire*
    kabriid
material alaab
materialism maadinimo
matter arrin
mattress furaash
maturation baaluq
mature qaan gaar
May maajo
mean dhabcaal
meander qalqalooc
means of production qalab

waxsoosaar
measles jadeeco
measurement cabbiraad
meat cad
medicine dawo
Mediterranean Sea Badda Cad
medium dhexyaal
medulla xidi maskaxeed
meet kulan
meeting shir
melt dhalaal
member xubin
membrane xuub
men niman
mend hagaaji
mend tol
meninges xuub maskaxeed
merchant ganacsade
mess qas
message farriin
metabolism dheefsasho
metal bir
metamorphic rock dhagax dhalan
    rogan
method dariiqo
mice jiirar
micro- ili-ma-aragto
midday duhur
middle badhtame; **to be in the**
    middle dhexee
midnight habeen badh
migrant labour shaq-raadin
    dibadeed
military base saldhig milatari
milk caano
milk an animal lis
milkman caanoole
million malyuun
mince up shiid
mind maskax; maan
mine *shaft* waxsyga; *explosive*
    miino
miner macdanqode
mineral(s) macdan
mineral salt cusbo macdaneed
minimum ugu yaraan
mining macdan qodis
minister wasiir; **foreign minister**
    wasiirka arrimaha dibadda
minority *ethnic* laan gaab; *political*
    laan gaab siyaasadeed

minute daqiiqad
mirror muraayad
miss seeg
missionary baadari
mist dhedo
mistake gef
mix qas
mixed farming qodaal dhafan
model isqurxi
modern cusub
molar gows
monarchy boqortooyo
Monday Isniin
money lacag
monkey daanyeer
monopoly iskukoob
monotheism alle keli aamine
monsoon mansuun
month bil
moon dayax
moral akhlaaq
morality anshax
more ka badan
morning aroor
mortar mooye
mosque masjid
mother hooyo
motion socod
motor dhaqaajiye
mountain buur
mouse doolli
mouth af
move dhaqaaji
movement dhaqdhaqaaq
much badan
mug koob
mule baqal
multiply isku dhufo
mumps qanjo barar
murder dil
murderer dile
muscle muruq
mushroom dooro waraabe; boqoshaa
music muusiko
mutton hilib idaad
mystical karaamo
myth sheeko baralay

N

nail *finger* ciddi; *metal* musmaar
name magac
narrow cidhiidhi
nasty xun
nation waddan
natural gas neef ceerin
nature dabiici
naughty edeb darro
navy ciidamma badda
near (to) dhow (u)
nearness ag
neat nidaamsan
neck luqun
necklace muriyad
need baahan
needle irbad
neighbor jaar
neighborhood agagaar
nest buul shimbireed
net shebeg
neutral dhexdhexaad
new cusub
news war; to give news (about) (ka) warran
newspaper jariidad
next dambe
nice wanaagsan
night habeen; to spend the night bari
nine sagaal
ninety sagaashan
no maya; may
no one cidna
node guntin
nodule gumud tare
noise buuq
nomads reer guuraa
nonsense bilaa micne
noon duhur
normal caadi
north waqooyi
nose san
note cod muusiko
notebook buug wax lagu qoro
nothing waxba
nourishing nuxurleh
nourishment nuxur
November Noofembar

now imminka
nucleus bu'
number nambar
nun baadariyad
nurse kalkaaliye
nut *metal* nadh; *food* laws
nutrition nafaqo
nylon nayloon

O

oasis war ileed
oats baarij
O.A.U. Ururka Midowga Afrika
occasion mar
occupation meherad
ocean badweyn
ocean floor sagxad badda
october oktoobar
of course! runtii!
oh! bal
oil saliid
ok! waa hagaag!
old da'weyn
old man oday
omnivorous geedo quute
on top of saaran
one *numeral* kow; *(used with a noun
    when one object is counted)* hal;
    *(used on its own when 'one'
    particular thing is referred to)*
    mid; *pronoun* la;
one of ka mid ah
oneself is
onion basal
open *verb* fur
open *adjective* furan
oppose hortag
opposite horjeed
opposition *political* mucaarad
oppression dulmi
oppressive dulmi badan
oppressor daallin
or ama
orange liin macaan
orbit majiire
order *noun* amar
order *verb* dalab
ordinary caadi

ore bir ceeriin
orient bari
oriental bari
orientation hagid
original asal
ostrich gorayo
other kale
ounce wiqiyad
output waxsoosaar
outside debed
ovary ugxanside
oven foorno
owl guumays
own la haansho
owner kii lahaa; hantiile

P

package bushqad
pact axdi; **to make a pact** wacatan
paddle batalaqsi
page baal
pail baaldi
pain xanuun
paint *noun* rinji
paint *verb* rinjiyee
paint brush burushka rinjiga
palace guri boqortooyo
palm calaacal
pan digsi
pancake canjeelo qalaad
pancreas baankiriyas
papaya babbay
paper warqad
parachute baarashud
parasite dulin
parcel bushqad
parent waalid
park beer raaxo
parliament barlamaan
parsley barataseemolo
part in
party *festive* xaflad; *political* xisbi
pass *noun* daw
pass *verb* dhaaf
pass along soo mar
pass by dhaaf

passenger rakaab
passport baasaboor
pasta baasto
paste cajiin
pastoral xoolo dhaqato
pasture daaq
patella kuraan
pattern naqshad
pavement waddo-cageed
paw cidiyo
pay noun mushahaar
pay verb bixi
pea salbuko
peace nabad; **peace be with you!** assalaamu calaykum!
peace-keeping nabad ilaalin
peace-keeping forces ciidammada ilaalinta
peacock daa'uus
peach fursuq
peak figta buurta
peanut laws
pear canbaruud
pebble quruurux
peck dhukubis
pedal dacsad makiinadeed
peel diir
peep dhugo
peg biin
pen qalin
pencil qalin qori
pendulum walhade
peninsula raasi
penny gambo
people dad
pepper capsicum berberooni; hot filfil
perhaps malaha
period kal
periodic kal-gal
permanent joogto ah
permeable habid
perpendicular ligan
persecution gowdhis
person qof
pestle kal
pet xayawaan guri joog ah
petal laace
petrol baansiin
pharynx dalqo
photocopy footookoobi

photograph sawir
photosynthesis footoosintasis
physical duleed
physical geography dhismaha jugraafiga duleed
piano buyaane
picture sawir
piece jab
pig doofaar
pigeon qooley
pigment midabsiis
pile kor saar
pilot duuliye
pillar tiir
pillow barkin
pin biin
pincers biinso
pinch qanjaruufo
pineapple cananaas
pink basali
pint dhucoyaray
pipe dhuun
pirate budhcad-badeed
pistil ubo-ubax
piston cabuudhiye
pit god
place meel
placenta mandheer
plain noun bannaan
plain adjective saafi
plait rablo
planet cir jooge
plankton sacaaf
plant noun beeritaan
plant verb beer
plantation qodaal
planting beerid
plants geedo
plaster jeesad
plastic caag
plate saxni; saxan
plateau dul
plates suxuun
play theater riwaayad
play verb ciyaar
please fadlan
plenty badan
pleural cavity moqor sanbabeed
pliers biinso
plot of land jago
plough cagafcagaf

plug balaag
plunge isku dhex tuur
pocket jeeb
poem gabay
point bar
pointed fiiqan
poison sun
polarity goborayn
pole cirif
politics siyaasad
pollen faxal
pollination faxlid
pond haro
pony faras yar
poor miskiin; faqiir
population tirada dadka
population census tiro koobka dadka
population density cufnaanta tirada dadka
population distribution filiqsanaanta dadka
porridge soor
port deked
porter xammaal
position goob
post office boosta
postcard booskaadh
postpone baaji
pot dheri
potato baradho
potential kayd
poultry xannaanadda digaaga
pour shub
powder daqiiq
power awood
praise amaan
pray ducaysi
prayer duco; salaad
prayer mat salli
preach wacdi
precious qaayo
precipitation roob
preface hordhac
prefer ka jeclayso
pregnant uur leh; xaamilo
prepare diyaargarow
prepare for u diyaargarow
prepared diyaar
present haddiyad
presenter (radio/TV) weriye

preserve kaydi
president madaxweyne
press *media* saxaafad
press *verb* riixo
pressure cadaadis; **air pressure** cadaadis hawo
pretend iska yeelyeel
pretty quruxsan
prevent baaji
previous hore
price sicir
pride isla weyni wacan
primary hore, horaad
prince ina boqor
princess ina boqor
principal maamule
principle mabda'
print daabac
printer madbacad
prison xabsi
prisoner maxbuus
private gaar ah
prize abaalgud
problem dhibaato
proceed soco
processing habaynta
producers soosaarayaal
production soosaarid
profession shaqo
profit faa'iido
program qorshe
progress horumar
progressive horusocod ah
projectile gantaal
promise ballanqaad
propagation baahid
property lahaansho; *characteristic* astaan
propose soo jeedi
prosper barwaaqo soor
prosperity barwaaqo-sooran
protect dhawr
protection ilaalin
protectorate mustacmarad
protein borotiin
protest banaanbax
protetariat borolataariyat
protoplasm brotobalaasam
proud qab dhaaf
prove caddee
provisions raashin

pulmonary aorta gar sambab
pump buufiye
pumpkin bocor
puree shii-shiid
purpose ujeeddo
purse kiish lacageed
pus malax
push riix
put dhig
put on top of saar
pyramid gunbur

Q

quality tayo
quantity tiro
quarrel dood
quarter rubuc; *area* xaafad
queen boqorad
question su'aal
queue saf
quick dhakhso
quiet aammus badan; **to be quiet** aammus
quinine kiniin
quiz kedis

R

rabbit bakayle
race *people* jinsi; qolo; *sport* tartan
radiation kaah
radiator raadyatoore
radio raydiyow
radio station rugta idaacadda
radioactive kaah-fal
radius gacan
rag calal
rage cadho; gadood; xanaaq
railroad waddo xadiid
railway tirayn
rain roob; da'
rainfall: annual rainfall roobka sanadka
rain gauge roob beeg
rain water xareed

rainbow qaanso
raise kici
raisins sabiib (madow)
ram wan
ranching ahminayn
range buuro silsilad ah
rank darajo
ransom madax furasho
rapid dhakhso badan
rare dhif
rascal ciyaala suuq
rat doolli
ratify oggolow
ravine tog
raw ceyriin; ceedhiin
raw material alaabo ceeriin
rays faalladho
razor sakiin
reach gaadh
read akhri
ready diyaar
real dhab
realize garo
really! wallaah!
rear dib
reason dar; sabab
reasonable macquul ah
receipt rasiidh
receive hel
recent waqti dhaw
reception goob xafladeed
recognition aqoonsi
recollect xasuus
recommend waani
record player mashiinka cajaladdaha
record rikoodh
recover dib u hel
red cas
Red Sea Badda Cas
red soil carro guduud
reduce dhin
reef shacaabi
refer tixraac
referee garsoore
reference tusmo khariidadeed
refine safee
reflection noqod
reform beddelid

refraction qaloocaan
refrigerator frinjideer; qaboojiye
refugee qaxooti
refuse diid
region gobol
register rajistar
regular habaysan
relation xidhiidh
relative khusayn
religion diin
repeat celi; ku celi
representative wakiil
repulsion kal-diid
residual buur haraa
resistance adkaysi
resolution go'aan
resonance isku dubadhac
respiration neefsasho
responsibility masuuliyad
rest nasasho
restaurant makhaayad
retrogressive dibusocod
return celi
revenue dakhli
revolution kacaan
revolve wareeg
rhinoceros wiyil
rice bariis
rich hodan
ride fuul
ridge laf
right midig; *correct* sax
right! waa hagaag!
ring fargal; kaatun
ripe bisil
rise kac
river webi
river course marinka webiga
river estuary biyo shub toosan
river source bilowga webiga
road dariiq
roast huuris
robe kurdad dheer; toob
rock dhadhaab; *igneous* dhadhaab
  shiileed; *metamorphic* dhadhaab
  dhalan rogan; *sedimentary*
  dhadhaab lakabeed
rocket sayruukh
roof saqaf
room qol
root xidid

rope xadhig
rotation wareeg
rough kala- dheer
round wareegsan
roundabout goolad baabuur
rub masax
rubber goomo
rubbish qashin
rude edeb darro
ruler mastarad
run orod
run (from) carar (ka)

S

sack kiish
sacrifice hurrid
sadness murugo
safety nabad gelyo
sailor badmaax
salary mushahaaro
salinity milixsanaan
salt cusbo
same isku mid
sand batax; cammuud
sap qori dheecaan
satellite dayax gacmeed
satisfied dheregsan; **to be satisfied**
  dhereg
saturation dheregsanaan
saturday sabti
sauce suugo
saucepan maddiibad
saucer seesar
savanna safaana
savings kayd
saw miishaar; miinshaar
scale qiyaas
scales miisaan
scar calaamad
scared: to be scared baqo
scarf masar
science saynis
scientist saynis yaqaan
scissors gaagaabiye; maqas

scooter mooto
scorpion dibqallooc
screw musmaar maraara leh
screwdriver dismis
sculpture quraar
school dugsi
sea bad; badda
sea level heerka badda
sea route dariiq badeed
season xilli
seat kursi
secondary dambe
secret sir
secretary xoghaye
security nabad sugid
see arag
seed iniin
seed selection abuur xulasho
seek raadi
segment xubin
segregate kalasoor
selection xulasho
self-determination aayo ka talin
self-government isxukun
sell gad
send dir
separately kala
September Sebtember
sesame sisin
set down deg
settle deg
settlement nagaadi
seven toddoba
seventy toddobaatan
sew tol
sewing machine harqaan
sewing toliin
sexual jinsi
shade hadh
shake ruxrux
shall doon
shape qaab
share qayb
shark libaax-badeed
sharp af-badan
shave xiiro
sheep ido
sheep & goats adhi
sheet go'
shelf khaanad
shell *sea* alleelo; *military* qashar

shepherd adhi-jire
shine birbiriq
ship markab
shirt shaadh(i)
shiver qadh-qadhyo
shoe kab
shoot toogo
shop dukaan
shopkeeper dukaanle
short gaaban
short circuit mareeg binis
short rains *(September to November)* dayr
shortness gaab
shorts surwaal gaaban
shoulder garab
shout qaylo
shovel majarafad
show *noun* riwaayad
show *verb* tus
shut xidh
shy khajilaad
sick jirran
side xag; **at the side of** agteeda
sieve miir
sign calaamad
silent aammusan
silk xariir
silt daad-wad
silly nacas
sing heesee
sing a song hees qaad
single keli
sink *noun* saxanka wax lagu mayro
sink *verb* deg
sip kabbo
siphon tuubo
sister walaal
sit down fadhiiso
sit fadhiisi
site goob
sitting room qolka fadhiga
six lix
sixty lixdan
size baaxad
skeleton saabka jidhka
skin maqaar
skip bood-bood
skip over iska dhaaf
skull laf madax
sky cir

slave addoon
slavery addoonsi
sleep hurdo
sleeping sickness cudur seexiye
sleeve gacanta shaadhka
slide sibiibixo
slip silbo
slipper dacas
slow gaabis
small yar
smell ur
smile ilka-caddee
smoke qiiq
smooth isku siman
snail xaaxeeyo
snake mas
snore khuuro
snow baraf
soap saabuun
social sciences cilmiga bulshada
socialist hantiwadaag
society bulsho
sock sharabaad
sofa soofe
soft jilicsan
soil conservation daryeelka carrada
soil erosion carro guur
soil fertilisation carro nafaqeyn
soil texture dunta ciida
solar system baho cadceedeed
soldier askari
solution milan
Somali *person* Soomaali
someone cid
son inan(ka)
song hees
sorghum hadhuudh
sound jabaq
soup maraq
sour dhanaan
source il
shave saami
south koonfur
sovereignty qarannimo
space hawada sare
spaceship gaadiidka hawada
spade majarafad
spaghetti baasto
spark plug dhimbiliye
speak hadal
spear waran

speed xawaare
spend bixi
spend the night in/at ku bari
spices xawaash
spicy basbaas leh
spider caaro
spinal nerve dareen farac xangule
spit candhuufo
spleen beeryar
sponge isbuunyo
spoon *metal* macalgad; *wooden* fandhaal
spore boodh
spokesman af hayeen
spray buufi
spring il
square afar gees
squirrel dabagaale
stable deggan
stairs jaranjar
stalk samay
stamp boolo
stand is taag
stand up toos
star xiddig
start bilow
start up kici
state *nation* dawlad; *condition* xaalad
station istaayshan
statistics cilmiga tirokoobka
stay deg
steel sulub
stem jirrid
step tallaabo
sternum sakaar
stick *noun* ul
stick *verb* xabag
still weli
sting mici
stir walaaq
stitch tolan
stock *food* fuud
stocking sharaabad xuub
stomach calool
stone dhagax
stool gambadh
stop joogso; *(someone/thing)* jooji
story sheeko
straight saani; **to be straight** hagaag
straighten hagaaji

straightness hagaag
strainer miir
stranger qalaad
strategic position meel istaraatiijika ah
straw caws
stream durdur
street dar iiq
stretch kala jiid
string xadhig
strong quwad
student ardey
submarine markabka quusa
submerge deg
subject maadad
succeed in guuleyso ku
success guuleysi, guul
suction pump buufiye nuuge
sugar sonkor
sugar cane qasab
suitcase shandad
sultana sabiib
sultanate boqortooyo
sun qorrax
Sunday Axad
sun rays fallaaraha qorraxda
sunrise qorrax soo bax
sunset qorrax dhac
supermarket macdaar weyn
superstition khuraafaad
supply base saldhigga saadka
supply siin
support taageero
suppose malee
sure hubaal ah
surface dul
surprised: to be surprised yaab
surrounded by ku wareegsan
surroundings agagaar
survey indha-indhayn
survive badbaad
suspension heehaab
suture tolan
swallow liq
sweat gland qanjidh dhidid
sweep fiiq
sweet noun macaan
sweet adjective macaan
swing leexo
sword seef
symbol summad

T

table miis
tablecloth maro-miis
tail dabo; dib
tailor dawaarlaha
take for oneself qaado
take from ka qaado
take qaad
take hold qabso
tale sheeko
talk hadal
talks wadahadallo
tall dheer
tank military dabbaabad; container haan
tanning migdayn
tap faucet baambad
tape cassette cajalad
tape recorder naastaro
tapeworm gooryaan mullaax
target shiish
taste dhadhan
taste bud ruqur dhadhan
taxi taksi
taxi driver tagsile
tea shaah
teach bar
teacher male macallin; female macallimad
teapot kidhli-shaah
tears ilmo
teashop makhaayad
technique tab
technology teknooloji
teeth ilko
telephone noun telefoon; telifoon
telephone (someone) verb telefoon (u) dir
compass diirad
television talifishan(ka)
television station rugta telefishanka
television antenna eeriyal
tell sheeg
temporary ku meel gaar ah
ten toban
tend xagli
tendon tahar
tension dareen

tent taandho
territory dhul
territorial expansion dhul balaarsi
terrorism argaggixiso
test ku day
thanked mahadsan
thanks be to God! Illaah mahaddi!
thank you mahadsanid
then dabadeedna
theory aragti
there halkaas
therefore sidaas darteed
thermometer heer kul sheeg
thermos flask termuus
thick adag
thief tuug
thigh bawdo
thin dhuuban
thing wax
think feker
thirst harraad
thirsty harraadsan
thirty soddon
this kan
thorn qodax
thought fikrad
thousand kun
thread dun
three saddex
throat hunguri
throw tuur
thumb suul
Thursday Khamiis
thyroid tayroodh
ticket tigidh
tie xidh; to be tied xidhan
time waqti; what time is it? waa
    immisadii?; at the same time isla
    markaasi; at that time markaas
tin qasacad
tiny dhibiq
tire *car* shaag
tired daal
tissue nud
toast roodhi duban
today maanta
toe faraha lugaha
together wada
tomato tamaandho
tomorrow berrito
tongue carrab

tool qalab
tooth ilig
tooth-stick caday
top dul
tortoise diin
touch taabo
tour wareeg
towards here soo
towel shukumaan
town magaalo
town centre farasmagaalo
townspeople reer magaal
toxin mariid
toy carruusad
tractor cagafcagaf
trachea hunguri cad
trade ganacsi
trade union urur shaqaale
trader gedisle
traffic gaadiid badan
training tababbar
travel safar
traveler socdaale
travelers socoto
treaty heshiis
tree geed
tree trunk jirrid
tribe qabiil
triumph guul
trousers surwaal
truck baabuur
trunk *tree* jirrid
truth run
try isku day
Tuesday Salaasa
turn leexo
twenty labaatan
twilight shaaca
twins mataano
two laba
typhoid jedeeco
tyre shaag

U

ugliness foolxumo
ugly foolxun
umbilical cord xuddun
umbrella dalaayad
U.N. *see* United Nations

unable

unable karaan la'aan
uncle *paternal* adeer; *maternal* abti
uncomfortable raaxo la'aan ah
unconsciousness miyir la'aan
underdevelopment dibudhac
underground dhusun
undo kala fur
undress dhar bixin
UNESCO Ururka UNESKO
uneven kala dheer dheer
unhappy farxad la'
unification mideyn
uniform direys
unit *of something* xabbad
unite midee
United Nations Qaraamada
   Midoobay
universal caan
university jaamacad
unkind naxariis la'aan ah
unload ka deji
unlucky nasiib darro
unpleasant karaahiyo
unripe ceyriin
untidy baali
until ilaa
up kor
up to ilaa
upper kore
upper arm cudud
upright toosan
upset cadho
urea yuuriya
urethra kaadi mareen
urgent deg-deg
urine kaadi
use adeegsi
used to jir
useful faa'iido leh
usefulness waxtar
useless faa'iido daran
usual caadi
usually sida caadiga ah
uterus ilmagaleen

V

vaccine; vaccination tallaal
valuable qiimo leh
values qiimo, qiyaam

valley dooxo; dry valley tog
van gaadhi qafilan
vanish libidh
vase dheri ubaxa
vegetable(s) khudrad
vegetation deegaan
vehicle gaadiid
vein arooro
venom waabay
vertical qoton
very aad . . . u
vest garan
vet dhakhtar xayawaanka
vicinity agagaar
victory guul
video fiidiyoow
village buulo; tuulo
villain budhcad
vine geedka canabka
vinegar khal
violent xoogahaan
virus feyruus
visa fiise
visit booqasho; booqo
vitamin(s) fiitamiin
voice cod
volcanic folkaaneed
vote cod
vowel shaqal
voyage safar
vulture geeltoosiye

W

waist dhex
wait kaadi u
wake up toos
wake someone up toosi
walk soco; lugee
wall derbi
want doon
war dagaal
wardrobe armaajo
warm diirraan
washing mashine mashiinka dharka
   lagu dhaqo
wasp jinac dulaa

watch *noun* saacad
watch *verb* eeg
water biyo
waterfall biyo dhac
water pot ashuun
watershed kala rog
water table heerka biyo gaadhka
water vapour uumi biyood
wave mawjad
wax dhukey
way si
weak daciif
wealth hodannimo
weapon hub
wear gashasho
weather cimilo-gooreed
weather forecast saadaasha hawada
weathering dhagax burbur
Wednesday Arbaca
weeds harame
week asbuuc; toddobaad
weep oohi
weigh miisaami
weight culays
welcome soo dhowee; **you're welcome!** adaa mudan!
welfare daryeelid
well *noun* ceel; **artesian well** ceelka aartiis
well *adjective* fiican
west galbeed
wet qoyan
whale nibiri
what max-; maxay
wheat sarreen
wheel shaag
where halkee
where? meeday?
which kee
which? kuma?
while intii
whisper xanshasheq
whistle foodhi
white caddaan
whole idil
why max- . . . u
why? waayo?
wide balaadhan
width ballaadh
wife afo; xaas

wife and children xaas
wig timo aan run ahayn
wild xayawaanka duur jooga ah
wild animals duur joog
wild dog yey
will doon
wish rabitaan
win guul
wind dabayl; **prevailing wind** dabayl joogto ah; **northeast tradewind** jiilaashin; **southwest tradewind** xagaashin
window diriishad
windward dabayl ku jeed
wings baalal
wink iljebi
winter jiilaal
wipe tirtir
wire silig
wisdom murti
wise caaqil
wish doon
with -leh
without -la'
wobble liic-liic
woman haweenay; naag; **young woman** gabadh
women dumar
wood *piece of wood* qori; *plank* loox; *firewood* xaabo; *forest* hawd
wool suuf
word eray
work *noun* hawl
work *verb* shaqee
worker shaqaale
world adduun; duni
World Bank Bangiga Adduunka
worm dirindiir
worry welwel
worship caabud
wrist curcur
write qor
wrong gef ah

X

x-ray khashaafad; raajo

Y

yam dun
yard daarad
yawn hamaansi
year sanad
yell qaylo
yes haa
yesterday shalay
yet weli
yogurt caano fadhi
yolk dhexda ukunta

you *singular* adiga
you *plural* idinka
young da'yar

Z

zero eber
zigzag qalqallooc
zip siib
zone jiida
zoo beerta xayawaanka

SOMALI
PHRASEBOOK

1. ETIQUETTE

Hello!	**Hayye!** or **Nabad!**
How are you?	**Iska warran?**
Fine, thank you.	**Waan fiicanahay.**
Good morning!	**Subax wanaagsan!**
Good afternoon!	**Galab wanaagsan!**
Good evening!	**Caweys wanaagsan!**
Good night!	**Habeen wanaagsan!**
See you tomorrow!	**Waa inoo berrito!**
Goodbye!	**Nabad gelyo!**
Bon voyage!	**Socdaal wanaagsan!**
Welcome!	**Soo dhowow!**

yes	**haa**
no	**maya**
thank you	**mahadsanid**
good luck!	**nasiib wanaagsan!**
excuse me!	**iga raalli ahow!***
	iga raalli ahaada!**
may I?	**miyaan karaa?**
sorry!	**waan ka xumahay!**

An Islamic greeting used everywhere and at any time of day or night is **Assalaamu calaykum!** 'Peace be with you!' — to which the response is **Calaykum assalaam!** 'And peace be with you!'

* Said to one person.
** Said to more than one.

2. QUICK REFERENCE

I	**aniga***
you	**adiga***
he; it	**isaga***
she; it	**iyada***
we *exclusive*	**annaga***
we *inclusive*	**innaga***
you *plural*	**idinka***
they	**iyaga***
this	**kan**
that	**kaas**
these	**kuwan**
those	**kuwaas**
here	**halkan**
there	**halkaas**
where?	**xaggee?**
who?	**kuma?** *or* **yaa?**
what?	**maxaa?**
when?	**goorma?**
which?	**-kee?/-tee?****
how?	**sidee?**
why?	**waayo?**
how far?	**fogaan intee le'eg?**
how much?	**waa intee?**
how many?	**immisa?**
what's that?	**waa maxay kaasi?**
is there?/are there?	**ma jiraa?** *or* **ma jiraan?**
how near?	**dhowaan intee ah?**
where is/are?	**mee?** *or* **meeye?**
what must I do?	**maxaan sameeyaa?**
what do you want?	**maxaad rabtaa?**
very	**aad ... u**
and	**iyo** *or* **oo**

* For other variants, see the Pronouns section on page 13.
** Used for masculine and feminine nouns respectively.

or	**ama;** *in questions* **mise**
but	**laakiin**
I like/want . . .	**Waan jeclahay/Waan doonayaa . . .**
I don't like/want . . .	**Ma jecli/Ma doonayo . . .**
I know.	**Waan ogahay.**
I don't know.	**Ma ogi.**
Do you understand?	**Ma fahamtaa?**
I understand.	**Waan fahmaa.**
I didn't understand.	**Maan fahmin.**
My condolences.	**Waan tacsiyadeynayaa.**
I am grateful.	**Waad mahadsantahay.**
It's important.	**Waa muhiim.**
It doesn't matter.	**Waxba ma laha.**
No problem!	**Dhib ma laha!**
more or less	**ha badnaato ama ha yaraato**
here is/are . . .	**halkan waxa jira . . .**
Is everything OK?	**Wax waliba sow ma wanaagsana?**
Danger!	**Khatar!**
How do you spell that?	**Sideen kaas u higgaadiyaa?**
I am . . .	**Waan . . .**
cold	**dhaxmoonayaa**
hot	**kululahay**
hungry	**gaajeysanahay**
thirsty	**harraadsanahay**
happy	**faraxsanahay**
sad	**cadheysanahay**
tired	**daalanahay**
well	**fiicanahay**
worried	**werwersanahay**
I am angry.	**Waan cadhaysnahay.**
I am right.	**Waa runtay.**
I am sleepy.	**Waan lu'loonayaa.**

2. INTRODUCTIONS

What is your name?	**Magacaa?**
My name is . . .	**Magacaygu waa . . .**
e.g. My name's Ahmad.	**Magacaygu waa Axmed.**
May I introduce you to . . .	**Ma iskiin baraa . . .**
e.g. May I introduce you to Ahmad.	**Ma iskiin baraa Ahmed.**
This is my. . .	**Kani waa. . .**
friend	**saaxiibkay**
colleague	**saaxiib shaqo-wadaag ah**
companion	**rafiiq**
relative	**ehel**

ABOUT YOURSELF . . .

NATIONALITY

Where are you from?	**Xaggeed ka timi?**
I am from. . .	**Waxaan ka imi. . .**
Australia	**Ustaraaliya**
Britain/England	**Biritayn/Iglan; Dalka Ingiriiska**
Canada	**Kanada**
Ireland	**Irlaand**
New Zealand	**Niyuu Siiland**
Northern Ireland	**Wuqooyiga Ayrlaand**
Wales	**Weylis**
Scotland	**Iskootlaand**
the USA	**Ameerika**
Germany	**Dalka Jarmalka**
France	**Dalka Faransiiska**
Italy	**Dalka Talyaaniga**
Europe	**Yurub**
India	**Hindiya**
Japan	**Jaabaan**

I am . . .	Waxaan ahay . . .
American	**Mareykan**
Australian	**Ustareeliyaan**
British/English	**Biritish/Ingiriis**
Canadian	**Kanadiyaan**
Irish	**Iyrash**
Welsh	**Walash**
Scottish	**Iskootish**
German	**Jarmal**
French	**Faransiis**
Italian	**Talyaani**

Where were you born?	**Xaggeed ku dhalatay?**
I was born in . . .	**Waxaan ku dhashay . . .**

HORN OF AFRICA PEOPLES

Somalian	**Soomaali**
Ethiopian	**Itiyoobiyaan**
Afar	**Canfar**
Amhara	**Amxaar**
Oromo	**Oroomo**
Kenyan	**Kiinyaan**
Sudanese	**Suudaani**
Eritrean	**Eritereyaan**

OCCUPATIONS

What do you do?	**Maxaad ka shaqaysaa?**
I am a/an . . .	**Waxa aan ahay . . .**
accountant	**xisaabiye**
administrator	**maamule**
agronomist	**beeryaqaan**
aid worker	**samo-fale**
architect	**ku xeel dheere arrimaha dhismaha**
artist	**fannaan**
business person	**baayac-mushtar**
carpenter	**nijaar**
consultant	**xeel dheer talo aqooneed laga qaato**
dentist	**dhakhtarka ilkaha**
diplomat	**danjire**
doctor	**dhakhtar**
economist	**dhaqaaleyahan**
engineer	**injineer**
farmer	**beeraley**
film-maker	**filim sameeye**
journalist	**suxufi**
lawyer	**looyar; garyaqaan**
manual worker	**gacan ku shaqeeye**
mechanic	**makaanik**
negotiator	**dhexdhexaadiye**
nurse	**kaalkaaliye; kal**
observer	**daawade**
officer worker	**xafiis ku shaqeeya**
pilot	**duuliye; baylood**
political scientist	**siyaasi yaqaan**
scientist	**saynisyahan**
secretary	**xoghaye**
soldier	**askari**
student	**arday**

surgeon	**dhakhtar ku takhasusay qalliinka**
teacher	**macallin; bare**
telecommunications specialist	**xeeldheere war-isgaadhsiinta ah**
tourist	**dalxiis**
training consultant	**xeeldheeraha ka talo bixinta tababarka**
writer	**qoraa**

AGE

How old are you?	**Immisa jir baad tahay?**
I am . . . years old.	**Waxaan ahay . . . jir.**

FAMILY

Are you married?	**Miyaad guursatey?**
I am single.	*male* **Waxaan ahay doob.**
	female **Waxaan ahay gashaanti.**
I am married.*	**Waxaan ahay xaas./Waan guursaday.**

Do you have a boyfriend?	**Saaxiib ma leedahay?**
Do you have a girlfriend?	**Saaxiibad ma leedahay?**
What is his/her name?	**Magaciis?/Magaceed?**
How many children do you have?	**Immisa carruur ah baad leedahay?**
I don't have any children.	**Carruur ma lihi.**
I have a daughter.	**Inan/gabadh baan leeyahay.**
I have a son.	**Inan/wiil baan leeyahay.**
How many sisters do you have?	**Immisa hablood baad walaalo tihiin?**
How many brothers do you have?	**Immisa wiil baad walaalo tihiin?**

* It is men only who actually say this. Women will define their marital status by context.

father	**aabbe**
mother	**hooyo**
grandfather	**awoowe**
grandmother	**ayeeyo**
brother	**walaal**
sister	**carruur**
child	**ilmo**
children	**carruur**
daughter	**inan; gabadh**
son	**inan; wiil**
twins	**mataano**
husband	**ninkayga**
wife	**naagtayda**
family	**xaas**
man	**nin**
woman	**gabadh; naag**
boy	**inan; wiil**
girl	**inan; gabadh**
person	**qof**
people	**dad**

RELIGION

Somalis are Sunni Muslims. Islam (**Islaam**) came early to the Horn of Africa through trade.

What is your religion?	**Diintee ayaad haysataa?**
I am (a) . . .	**Waxaan ahay . . .**
Muslim	**muslim**
Buddhist	**buudhiist**
Orthodox	**ortodhogos**
Christian	**kiristaan; masiixi**
Hindu	**hinduu**
Jewish	**yuuhuudi**

I am not religious.	**Waxaan ahay bilaa-diin.**

4. LANGUAGE

Aside from other indigenous languages spoken in the Horn of Africa, many Somalis will speak a little Arabic while some in the south may speak Swahili. Some will also know at least a smattering of one or more European languages like Italian and English.

Do you speak English?	**Af Ingriisi ma ku hadli kartaa?**
Do you speak Somali?	**Af Soomaali ma ku hadli kartaa?**
Do you speak Italian?	**Af Talyaani ma ku hadli kartaa?**
Do you speak German?	**Af Jarmal ma ku hadli kartaa?**
Do you speak French?	**Af Faransiis ma ku hadli kartaa?**
Do you speak Arabic?	**Af Carbeed ma ku hadli kartaa?**

Does anyone speak English?	**Qofna Af Ingriisi ma ku hadli karaa?**
I speak a little . . .	**In yar baan ku hadlaa . . .**

I don't speak. . .	**Kuma hadlo . . .**
I understand.	**Waan fahmaa.**
I don't understand.	**Maan fahmo.**

Please point to the word in the book.	**Fadlan kelmedda buug iiga dhex calaamadi.**
Please wait while I look up the word.	**Fadlan i sug intaan kelmeda eegayo.**
Could you speak more slowly, please?	**Fadlan miyir ma u hadli kartaa?**
Could you repeat that?	**Igu celi?**

How do you say . . . in Somali?	**Sidee Af Soomaali . . . loogu yidhaahdaa?**
What does . . . mean?	**Eraygii . . . macnihiisu waa maxay?**
How do you pronounce this word?	**Sidee baa loogu dhawaaqaa ereygan?**

I speak . . .	**Waxa aan ku hadlaa . . .**
Amharic	**Af Xabashi**
Arabic	**Af Carbeed**
Danish	**Af Dheenish**
Dutch	**Af Holandish**
English	**Af Ingriisi**
French	**Af Faransiis**
German	**Af Jarmal**
Greek	**Af Giriig**
Italian	**Af Talyaani**
Japanese	**Af Jabaaniis**
Portuguese	**Af Boortiqiis**
Russian	**Af Ruush**
Spanish	**Af Isbaanish**
Swahili	**Af Sawaaxili**
Tigrinya	**Af Tigre**
Turkish	**Af Turki**

5. BUREAUCRACY

Note that some forms you encounter may be written in Arabic as well as Somali.

FILLING IN FORMS

name	**magac**
address	**cinwaan**
date of birth	**maalintaad dhalatay**
place of birth	**meesha aad ku dhalatay**
nationality	**dhalashadaada**
age	**da'daada**
sex: male	**lab**
female	**dheddig**
religion	**diintaada**
reason for travel:	**sababta socdaalkaaga:**
business	**baayacmushtar**
tourism	**dalxiis**
work	**shaqo**
personal	**arrin gaar ahaaneed**
profession	**shaqo gaar**
date	**taariikh**
date of arrival	**maalintaad timi**
date of departure	**maalintaad dhooftay**
passport	**baasaaboor**
passport number	**lambarka baasaaboorka**
visa	**fiise**
currency	**lacag**

MINISTRIES

Ministry of Defense	**Wasaaradda Difaaca**
Ministry of Agriculture	**Wasaaradda Beeraha**
Ministry of Home Affairs	**Wasaaradda Arrimaha Gudaha**

Ministry of Foreign Affairs	**Wasaaradda Arrimaha Dibadda**
Ministry of Transport	**Wasaaradda Gaadiidka**
Ministry of Health	**Wasaaradda Caafimaadka**
Ministry of Education	**Wasaaradda Waxbarashada**
Ministry of Justice	**Wasaaradda Cadaaladda**

USEFUL PHRASES

Is this the correct form?	**Sidani ma sida saxa ah baa?**
What does this mean?	**Macneheedu waa maxay?**
Where is . . . 's office?	**Waa xaggee xafiiska . . . ?**
Which floor is it on?	**Waa dabaqee?**
Does the lift work?	**Wiishku ma shaqaynayaa?**
Is Mr./Ms. . . . in?	**Mr./Ms. . . . ma joogaa?**
Please tell him/her that I am here.	**Fadlan u sheeg inaan joogo.**
I can't wait, I have an appointment.	**Ma sugi karo waayo ballan kale ayaan leeyahay.**
Tell him/her that I was here.	**U sheeg inaan joogay.**

6. TRAVEL

Public transport ('Gaadiidka dadweynaha') — When running, buses are generally too crammed to be practical. Far more practical are taxis which you can hail in the street. Bicycles or motorbikes may be found for personal use.

ENQUIRIES

What time does (the) . . . leave/arrive?	**Goorma . . .**
the airplane	**ayay diyaaraddu tegeysaa/ imanaysaa?**
the boat	**ayay doonnidu tegeysaa/ imanaysaa?**
the bus	**ayuu basku tegeyaa/imanayaa?**
the train	**ayuu tareenku tegeyaa/imanayaa?**
The plane is delayed/ cancelled.	**Diyaaraddii dib bay u dhacday.**
The train is delayed/ cancelled.	**Diyaaraddii way baaqatay.**
How long will it be delayed?	**Intee ayuu dib u dhacayaa?**
There is a delay of . . . hours.	**Waxa uu dib u dhacayaa . . . saacadood.**

BUYING TICKETS

Excuse me, where is the ticket office?	**Adigoo iga raali ah ma ii sheegi kartaa xafiiska tigidhaha?**
Where can I buy a ticket?	**Xaggee ayaan tigidh ka soo iibsan karaa.**
I want to go to. . .	**Waxaan rabaa inaan tago . . .**
I want a ticket to . . .	**Waxaan rabaa tigidh ku siman . . .**
I would like . . .	**Waxaan rabaa . . .**
a one-way ticket	**tigidh tegitaan kaliya ah**
a return ticket	**tigidh soo noqosho ah**
first class	**tigidh feeras kalaas ah**
second class	**tigidh sekond kalaas ah**
business class	**tigidh bisnes kalaas ah**

Do I pay in dollars or shillings?	**Doolar mise shilin midkee baan ku bixin karaa?**
You must pay in dollars.	**Waa inaad doolar ku bixiso.**
You must pay in shillings.	**Waa inaad shilin ku bixiso.**
You can pay in either.	**Kaad doonto waad ku bixin kartaa.**
Can I reserve a place?	**Kursi ma ii hayn kartaa?**
How long does the trip take?	**Socdaalkanu intee ayuu qaadan doonaa?**
Is it a direct route?	**Ma duulimaad toos ah baa?**

AIR

Is there a flight to . . . ?	**Ma jiraa duulimaad . . . ahi?**
When is the next flight to . . . ?	**Duulimaadka kan ku xigee . . . goorma ayaa yahay?**
How long is the flight?	**Duulimaadkan dhererkiisu xaggee ku egyahay?**
What is the flight number?	**Nambarka duulimaadku waa maxay?**
You must check in at . . .	**Waa in aad ka jeeggareyso . . .**
Is the flight delayed?	**Duulimaadkii ma dib buu u dhacay?**
How many hours is the flight delayed?	**Immisa saacadood buu dib u dhacay?**
Is this the flight for . . . ?	**Duulimaadkani ma ku socdaa . . . ?**
Is that the flight from . . . ?	**Duulimaadkan diyaaradu ma ka timi . . . ?**
When is the Rome flight arriving?	**Rooma diyaaradii ka imanaysey goormay timaaddaa?**
Is it on time?	**Wakhtigeedu ma mid sugan baa?**
Is the flight late?	**Duulimaadkii miyuu raagay?**
Do I have to change planes?	**Diyaarado kale ma ku beddelayaa?**

Has the plane left Rome yet?	**Diyaaraddii miyay weli Rooma ka soo dhaaftay?**
What time does the plane take off?	**Goorma ayay diyaaradu kacaysaa?**
What time do we arrive in Rome?	**Xillima ayaanu Rooma gaadhaynaa?**
excess baggage	**culays dheeraad**
international flight	**duulimaad caalami ah**
internal flight	**duulimaad dalka gudiihiisa ah**

BUS

bus stop	**bas istob**
Where is the bus stop/station?	**Waa xaggee bas istobtu/isteeshinka basku?**
Take me to the bus station.	**I gee isteeshinka baska?**
Which bus goes to . . . ?	**Baskee baa tegeya . . . ?**
Does this bus go to . . . ?	**Baskani miyuu tegeyaa . . . ?**
What time is the . . . bus?	**Goorma ayuu tegeyaa baska/baskan . . . ?**
next	**ku xigaa**
first	**ugu horeeyaa**
last	**ugu dambeeyaa**
Will you let me know when we get to . . . ?	**Ma ii sheegi kartaa goorta aynu gaadhno . . . ?**
Stop, I want to get off!	**Ii jooji, waxaan rabaa inaan dego!**
Where can I get a bus to . . . ?	**Xaggee ayaan ka heli karaa baska tegaaya . . . ?**
When is the first bus to . . . ?	**Waa goorma goorta baska ugu horreeyaa uu tegi doono . . . ?**
When is the last bus to . . . ?	**Waa goorma goorta baska ugu dambeeyaa uu tegi doono . . . ?**
When is the next bus to . . . ?	**Waa goorma goorta uu baskan ka xigaa uu tegi doonaa . . . ?**
Do I have to change buses?	**Ma basas kale ayaan ku baddelayaa?**

I want to get off at . . .	**Waxa aan rabaa inaan ku dego . . .**
Please let me off at the next stop.	**Fadlan ii ogoloow inaan istobtan istobta ku xigta ku dhaadhaco.**
Please let me off here.	**Fadlan ii ogoloow inaan halkan ku hadho.**
How long is the journey?	**Waa intee dhererka socdaalkani?**
What is the fare?	**Kiradu/nooligu waa immisa?**
I need my luggage, please.	**Fadlan shandadahaygii baan rabaa.**
That's my bag.	**Taasi waa shandadaydii**

TRAIN

Passengers must. . .	**Rakkaabka waa in ay . . .**
change trains.	**beddelaan tareenka**
change platforms.	**beddelaan balaadfoomka**
Is this the right platform for . . . ?	**Ma yahay kani balaadfoomkii saxa ahaa ee tareenka ku socda . . . ?**
The train leaves from platform . . .	**Tareenku wuxuu ka baxayaa balaadfoomka lambarka . . .**
Is there a timetable?	**Halkan ma jiraa jadwalka laga eegto tareemada socdaalkoodee?**
Which platform should I go to?	**Balaadfoomkeen ka raagi karaa tareenka tegaya . . . ?**
platform one/two	**balaadfoomka koobaad/ labaad**
You must change trains at . . .	**Waa in aad tareenka ku bedesho . . .**
Where can I buy tickets?	**Halkee baan tigidhada ka goosan karaa?**
Will the train leave on time?	**Tareenku xillii sugan miyuu ku dhaqaaqayaa?**

| There will be a delay of minutes. | **Waxa jira dibu dhac daqiiqado ah.** |
| There will be a delay of . . . hours. | **Dib u dhac . . . saacadood ah baa jira.** |

TAXI

Some taxis are marked , while others are not. You can also wave down and negotiate a fare with any private car willing to go your way, although this is not always as safe. To avoid unpleasant surprises, agree to fares in advance. It is useful to be able to tell the driver your destination in Somali (or have it written down on a piece of paper). Be warned, however, that some drivers will have as little idea as you as to the precise whereabouts of your destination.

Taxi!	**Tagsi!**
Where can I get a taxi?	**Halkee baan tagsi ka heli karaa?**
Please could you get me a taxi.	**Fadlan tagsi mayla raadin kartaa?**
Can you take me to. . . ?	**Ma i geyn kartaa . . . ?**
Please take me to . . .	**Fadlan i gee . . . ?**
How much will it cost it to. . . ?	**Immisa weeye nooligu/ kiradu ilaa . . . ?**
To this address, please.	**Fadlan cinwaankan i gee.**
Turn left.	**Bidix u leexo.**
Turn right.	**Midig u leexo.**
Go straight ahead.	**Toos u soco.**
Stop!	**Joogso!; Is taag!**
Don't stop!	**Ha joogsan!; Ha is taagin!**
I'm in a hurry.	**Waan degdegsanahay.**
Please drive more slowly!	**Fadlan sidan si ka gaabinaysa gaadhiga u wad!**
Here is fine, thank you.	**Halkan baa wanaagsan mahadsanid.**
The next corner, please.	**Fadlan koonaha/geeska dambe i gee.**
The next street to the left.	**Jidka kale ee bidixda.**

The next street to the right.	**Jidka kale ee midigta.**
Stop here!	**Halkan ii jooji!**
Stop the car, I want to get out.	**Gaadhiga jooji halkan baan bixi rabaa.**
Please wait here.	**Fadlan halkan igu sug.**
Take me to the airport.	**Gegida diyaaradaha i gee.**

GENERAL PHRASES

I want to get off at . . .	**Waxaan rabaa inaan ku dego . . .**
Excuse me!	**Iga raalli ahow!**
Excuse me, may I get by?	**Iga raalli ahow, ma dhaafi karaa?**
These are my bags.	**Kuwaasi waa shandadahaygii.**
Please put them there.	**Fadlan halkaas dhig.**
Is this seat free?	**Kursiganu miyuu bannaanyahay?**
I think that's my seat.	**Waxa aan filayaa inuu yahay kursigaygii.**

EXTRA WORDS

ambulance	**ambalaas**
bicycle	**baaskeel**
boat	**doonni**
car	**gaadhi**
4-wheel drive	**foor wiildarayf**
helicopter	**helikobtar**
horse & cart	**faras iyo carabiyad**
motorbike	**dhugdhugley**
trolley bus	**bas**
airport	**garoonka diyaaradaha/ gegida diyaaradaha**
airport tax	**cashuurta gegida diyaaradaha**
arrivals	**cagadhigasho**
baggage counter	**barta maamulka rarka iyo rogida xamuulka**
boarding pass	**boordhin baas**

bus stop	**bas istob**
cancellation	**baaqasho**
check-in counter	**kaawntarka ka hubi**
check-in	**hubi**
closed	**xidhan**
customs	**xafiiska cashuuraha/kastam**
delay	**dib u dhac**
departures	**duulid**
emergency exit	**iridka degdeg ah**
entrance	**iridka gelitaanka**
exit	**iridka bixitaanka**
express	**degdeg ah**
ferry	**feeri**
information	**macluumaad**
ladies/gents	**suuli dumarka/suuli ragga**
local (for trains)	**tareenka gudaha**
no entry	**lama-geli karo**
no smoking	**sigaarka laguma cabi karo**
open	**furan**
path	**jid lugeed**
platform number	**lambarka balaadfoomka**
railway	**jidka tareenka/xadiidka**
reserved	**kaydsan**
road	**jid; waddo**
sign	**calaamad**
sleeping car	**gaadhiga lagu seexdo**
station	**istayshin; maxaddad**
telephone	**tilifoon**
ticket office	**xafiiska tigidhada**
timetable	**jadwal**
toilets	**baytalmayo**
town center	**faras-magaale**
train station	**maxaddadda tareenka; isteeshinka tareenka**

7. ACCOMMODATION

Aside from the main hotels, you will find that room service is not always available, and breakfast or other meals will have to be negotiated and paid for separately.

I am looking for a . . .	**Waxaan doonayaa . . .**
guesthouse	**guri martiyeed**
hotel	**albeerko; huteel**
hostel	**hostal**

Is there anywhere I can stay for the night?	**Meelahan ma jirtaa meel aan caawa u hoydaa?**
Is there anywhere we can stay for the night?	**Meelahan ma jirtaa meel aannu caawa u hoyannaa?**

Where is . . . ?	**Xaggee buu jiraa . . . ?**
a cheap hotel	**huteel jabani**
a good hotel	**huteel wanaagsani**
a nearby hotel	**huteel dhawi**
a clean hotel	**huteel nadiifsani**
What is the address?	**Maxuu yahay cinwaanku**
Could you write the address please?	**Fadlan cinwaanka ma ii qori kartaa?**

AT THE HOTEL

Do you have any rooms free?	**Ma helaysaa qolal bannaan?**
I would like . . .	**Waxa aan doonayaa . . .**
a single room	**qol singal ah/nafar ah**
a double room	**qol laba nafar ah**
We'd like a room.	**Waxaanu rabnaa qol.**
We'd like two rooms.	**Waxaanu rabnaa laba qol.**
I want a room with . . .	**Waxan rabaa qol leh . . .**
a bathroom	**baad**
a shower	**shaawar; rushaashad**
a television	**telefishan**

a window	**daaqad**
a double bed	**sariir laba nafar qaad ah**
a balcony	**balakoono**
I want a room that's quiet.	**Waxaanu rabaa qol bilaa sanqadh ah.**
How long will you be staying?	**Intee ayaad degganaan doontaa?**
How many nights?	**Immisa habeen?**
I'm going to stay for . . .	**Waxa aan degganaan doonaa . . .**
one day	**maalin**
two days	**laba maalmood**
one week	**hal toddobaad**
Do you have any I.D.?	**Ma haysataa wax caddayn ah?**
Sorry, we're full.	**Waan ka xumahay hudheelku wuu buuxaa.**
I have a reservation.	**Qol baan sii ballansaday.**
My name is . . .	**Magacaygu waa . . .**
May I speak to the manager please?	**Fadlan maareeyaha ma la hadli karaa?**
I have to meet someone here.	**Halkan qof baan kula ballansanahay.**
How much is it per night?	**Habeenkii waa immisa?**
How much is it per person?	**Qofkii waa immisa?**
How much is it per week?	**Wiiggii*/todobaadkii* waa immisa?**
It's . . . per day.	**Maalintii kiradu waa . . .**
It's . . . per person.	**Qofkii kiradu waa . . .**
Can I see it?	**Ma arki karaa?**
Are there any others?	**Kuwo kale ma jiraan?**
Is there . . . ?	**Ma leeyahay . . . ?**
air conditioning	**qaboojiye**
laundry service	**dhar dhaqidi**
room service	**qolkoo laguugu shaqeeyo**
a telephone	**tilifoon**
hot water	**biyo kulul**

* Both mean 'week.'

No, I don't like it.	**Maya ma jecli.**
It's too . . .	**Aad bay u . . .**
cold	**qabawdahay**
hot	**kulushahay**
big	**weyntahay**
dark	**madowdahay**
small	**yartahay**
noisy	**sanqadh-badan tahay**
dirty	**uskag ah; wasakh ah**

It's fine, I'll take it.	**Way wanaagsantahay, waan qaadan doonaa.**
Where is the bathroom?	**Mee baadku?**
Is there hot water all day?	**Biyo kululi ma jiraan maalintii oo dhan?**
Do you have a safe?	**Khasnad ma leedahay?**
Is there anywhere to wash clothes?	**Ma jirtaa meel dharka lagu maydhaa?/ qasaali karaa?/dhaqaa?**
Can I use the telephone?	**Telifoonkan ma isticmaali karaa?**

NEEDS

I need . . .	**Waxaan u baahanahay . . .**
candles	**shamac**
toilet paper	**waraaqaha saxarotirka; tooyled beebar**
soap	**saabuun**
clean sheets	**go'yaal nadiif ah**
an extra blanket	**buste dheeraad ah**
drinking water	**biyo cabitaan**
a light bulb	**guluubka laydhka/nalka**
Please wake me up at . . . (o'clock).	**Fadlan i toosi . . . subaxnimo.**
Please change the sheets.	**Fadlan iga beddel go'yaasha.**

I can't open/close the window.	**Ma furi karo/xidhi karo daaqadda.**
I have lost my key.	**Furahaygii baa iga lumay.**
Can I have the key to my room?	**Furaha qolkayga ma haysan karaa.**
The toilet won't flush.	**Baytalmayga biyihiisa wasakhda qaadayaa ma shaqaynayaan.**
I am leaving now.	**Imminkaan tegeyaa.**
We are leaving now.	**Imminkaanu tegeynaa.**
I would like to pay the bill.	**Waxaan doonayaa inaan kharashka bixiyo.**
I would like to be woken up at . . . (o'clock).	**Waxaan jeclaan lahaa in la i toosiyo . . .**
The water has been cut off.	**Biyuhu wuu go'anyahay.**
The electricity has been cut off.	**Laydhku wuu go'anyahay.**
The gas has been cut off.	**Gaastu way go'antahay.**
The air conditioning doesn't work.	**Hawo qaboojintu ma shaqaynayso.**
The heater doesn't work.	**Kulsiintu ma shaqeynayso.**
The phone doesn't work.	**Tilifoonku ma shaqaynayo.**
I can't flush the toilet.	**Biyaha qaadista wasakhda ee baytalmaygu ma shaqaynayaan.**
The toilet is blocked.	**Baytalmaygu wuu oodanyahay.**
I can't switch off the tap.	**Qasabadda ma xidhi karo.**

EXTRA WORDS

bathroom	**baad; musqul**
bed	**sariir**
bill	**xisaab**
blanket	**buste**
candle	**shamac**
chair	**kursi**

clean	**nadiifsan**
cold water	**biyo qabow**
cupboard	**kabadh**
dark	**madow**
dirty	**uskag; wasakh**
doorlock	**handaraab**
double bed	**sariir laba nafar ah**
electricity	**laydha**
excluded	**ka debedda**
fridge	**qaboojiye**
hot/cold	**kulayl/qabow**
hot water	**biyo kulul**
included	**ku jiraan**
key	**fure**
laundry	**doobbiile**
mattress	**barkimo**
meals	**waqtiyada cuntada**
mirror	**muraayad**
name	**magac**
noisy	**sanqadh badan**
padlock	**quful**
pillow	**barkin**
plug	**balaag**
quiet	**deggan**
room	**qol**
room number	**qolka nambarkiisa**
shampoo	**shaanboo**
sheet	**go'**
shower	**rushaashad; shaawar**
suitcase	**samsanaayt; shandad**
surname	**magaca awoowga**
table	**miis**
towel	**tuwaal**
water	**biyo**
window	**daaqad**

8. FOOD & DRINK

Food plays an important part of Somali life, and important events in all aspects of life and the seasons are marked with a feast of one form or another. Dishes on offer will vary from region to region and from season to season.

breakfast	**quraac**
lunch	**qado**
snack	**cuwaaf**
dinner, supper	**casho**
dessert	**macmacaan**

I'm hungry.	**Waan gaajoonayaaa.**
I'm thirsty.	**Waan harraadsanahay.**

Ramadan	**Ramadaan; Ramadhaan**
I am fasting.	**Waan soomanahay.**
to break a fast	**afur**

Do you know a good restaurant?	**Ma garanaysaa makhaayad wanaagsan?**
I would like a table for . . . please.	**Fadlan waxaan doonayaa miis . . . qof qaada.**

Can I see the menu please?	**Fadlan menyuuga i sii?**
I'm still looking at the menu.	**Menyuuga weli ayaan eegayaa.**
I would like to order now.	**Imminka ayaan wax dalbanayaa.**
What's this?	**Kani waa maxay?**
Is it spicy?	**Ma besbaas buu leeyahay?**
Does it have meat in it?	**Hilib miyuu ku jiraa?**
Does it have alcohol in it?	**Isbiirto miyaa ku jirtaa?/ Khamri miyaa ku jirtaa?**

Do you have . . . ?	**Ma haysaa . . . ?**
We don't have . . .	**Ma hayno . . . ?**
What would you recommend?	**Maxaad ii soo jeedinaysaa?**
Do you want . . . ?	**Ma rabtaa . . . ?/Doonaysaa . . . ?**
Can I order some more . . . ?	**Ma dalban karaa . . . kale?**
That's all, thank you.	**Waa dhantahay mahadsanid.**
That's enough, thanks.	**Intaas baa igu filan mahadsanid.**
I haven't finished yet.	**Weli maan dhammaysan.**
I have finished eating.	**Cuntadaydii waan dhammaystay.**
I am full up!	**Waan dhergey!**
Where are the toilets?	**Mee baytalmaygu?**
I am a vegetarian.	**Khudrad cune ayaan ahay.**
I don't eat meat.	**Hilibka ma cuno.**
I don't eat pork.	**Doofaarka ma cuno.**
I don't eat chicken or fish.	**Digaaga ama kalluunka ma cuno.**
I don't drink alcohol.	**Khamriga ma cabbo.**
I don't smoke.	**Sigaarka ma cabbo.**
I would like . . .	**Waxaan rabaa . . .**
an ashtray	**haashtari**
the bill	**xisaabta**
a glass of water	**koob biyo ah**
a bottle of water	**quraarad biyo ah**
a bottle of wine	**quraarad waayn ah**
a bottle of beer	**quraarad biire ah**
another bottle	**quraarad kale**
a bottle-opener	**manfag**

EXTRA WORDS

a corkscrew	**manfag**
a cup	**bakeeri; koob**
dessert	**macmacaan**
a drink	**cabbitaan**
a fork	**farogeeto**
another chair	**kursi kale**
another plate	**bilaydh/saxan kale**
another glass	**bakeeri kale**
another cup	**koob kale**
a napkin	**istiraasho**
a glass	**bakeeri**
a knife	**mindi**
a plate	**bilaydh; saxan**
a spoon	**malqacad**
table	**miis**
teaspoon	**malqacadda shaaha**
toothpick	**findhicil**

fresh	**daray**
spicy	**besbaas**
stale	**cunto xumaaday**
sour	**dhanaan**
sweet	**macaan**
hot	**kulayl**
cold	**qabow**
salty	**milix badan**
tasteless	**bilaa-dhadhan**
bad	**xun**
tasty	**dhadhan leh**

too much	**aad u badan**
too little	**aad u yar**
not enough	**kuma filma**

FOOD

bread	**roodhi**
cheese	**jiis**
chewing gum	**xanjo**
egg	**beed; ukun**
flour	**daqiiq**
french fries	**baradho shiilan**
honey	**malab**
ice cream	**iskiriin**
ketchup	**kajab**
nut	**loos**
oil	**saliid**
pasta	**baasto**
pepper	**basbaas**
sweet pepper	**barbarooni**
rice	**bariis**
salad	**saladh**
salt	**cusbo**
sandwich	**saanwij**
soup	**maraq**
sugar	**sonkor**
candy	**nacnac**
vinegar	**khal**
yogurt	**ciir; gadhoodh**

VEGETABLES

potato	**baradho**
tomato	**tamaandho**
vegetables	**khudaar**
yam	**baradho macaan**

FRUIT

apple	**tufaax**
banana	**moos**
coconut	**qumbe**
date	**timir**

FOOD & DRINK

fig	**tiin**
grape	**canab**
lemon	**liin dhanaan**
melon	**shamaam; bartiikh**
orange	**liin macaan**
pineapple	**cananaas**
watermelon	**xabxab; qare**

MEAT

beef	**hilib lo'aad**
chicken	**digaag**
fish	**kalluun**
lamb	**wan**
meat	**hilib**
pork	**doofaar**
sausage	**soosayj**

DRINK

Remember to ask for modern soft drinks by brand name.

alcohol	**khamri**
bottle	**quraarad**
brandy	**barandhi**
can	**qasacad**
coffee	**bun; kaafi**
coffee with milk	**bun caano leh**
fruit juice	**casiir**
ice	**baraf**
milk	**caano**
mineral water	**biyo macdanaysan**
tea	**shaah**
tea with lemon	**shaah liin dhanaan leh**
tea with milk	**shaah caano leh**
no sugar, please	**fadlan sonkor ha ku soo darin**
vodka	**foodke**

| whisky | **wiski** |
| wine | **waayn** |

MORE ON FOOD & DRINK

Somalis produce a wide range of seasonal grains and vegetables, including **sonkorqan** 'yam,' **muus** 'bananas,' **bocor** 'squashes,' **diir/digir** 'beans/peas,' **basal** 'onion,' **qassab** 'sugar cane,' **loows** peanuts,' **hadhuudh** 'sorghum,' **moxoggo** 'cassava/manioc' and **sinasim** 'sesame.' Added to these are the meat and other products that come from the herds of camels, cows, sheep and goats traditionally kept on the land.

A traditional main meal may be centered around **soor**, a 'porridge' made from a variety of grains such as maize (**gallay**), wheat (**sarreen**) or even rice (**bariis**) — or two can be added together, like maize and coconut (**qumbe**) or wheat and peas, etc. Stews (**sanuunad**) can be made from goat meat, beef, mutton, fish, rice, or pasta (**baasto**). Many dishes add garlic (**toon**), salt (**cusbo**), and more than a dash of hot chilli pepper (**basbaas**) — food that is spicy or hot is called **basbaas leh**. There are also soups (**maraq**), which also tend to be spicy.

There are two words for eggs: **ugxan** (*singular* **ugax**) means eggs in general, while **ukumo** (*singular* **ukun**) is used specifically for chicken eggs.

Traditional drinks include camel milk (**caano geel**) and Somali tea (**shaah**), which is made by brewing tea, sugar, milk, and spices (**xawaash**) such as cinnamon (**qorfe**), cardamom (**heyl**), cloves (**dhegayare**), and black pepper (**filfil**). And you might round off your meal with fresh dates (**timir**).

Although fish (**kalluun**) has never been a part of Somalis' traditional diet despite their long coastline, campaigns have been launched to promote fish and fishing.

When Somalis sit down and are about to eat, they say **"Bismillaah!"** — "In the name of God!"

9. DIRECTIONS

Where is . . . ?	**Waa xaggee . . . ?**
the art gallery	**rugta bandhigga farshaxanka**
a bank	**baanku/bangigu**
the church	**kiniisaddu**
the Ministry of . . .	**wasaarada . . .**
the mosque	**masaajidku**
the city center	**faras magaaluhu**
the . . . embassy	**safaaradda . . .**
my hotel	**huteelkaygu**
the market	**suuqu**
the museum	**guriga carwadu**
the police	**booliisku**
the post office	**xafiiska boostadu**
a toilet	**tooyladku; baytalmaygu**
the consulate	**qunsuliyaddu**
the telephone center	**rugta dhexe ee tilifoonadu**
an information office	**xafiiska macluumaadku**
the parliament	**guriga baarlamaanku**
the university	**jaamacaddu**
the airport	**gegida diyaaraduhu**
the station	**isteyshinku**
the academy	**kuliyaddu**

What . . . is this?	**Muxuu yahay . . . ?** *masculine words*
bridge	**biriishkani**
building	**dhismahani**
river	**webigani**
What . . . is this?	**Maxay tahay . . . ?** *feminine words*
district	**degmadani**
road	**waddadani**
street	**wadiiqadani**
suburb	**xaafaddani**
town	**magaaladani**
village	**tuuladani**

What is this building?	**Muxuu yahay dhismahani?**
What is that building?	**Muxuu yahay dhismahaasi?**
What time does it open?	**Xillima ayaa la furaa?**
What time does it close?	**Xillima ayaa la xidhaa?**
Can I park here?	**Halkan gaadhiga ma dhigan karaa?**
Are we on the right road for . . . ?	**Ma haysanaa jidkii saxa ah ee tegaya . . . ?**
How many kilometers is it to . . . ?	**Immisa kiiloomitir bay . . . jirtaa?**
It is . . . kilometers away.	**Waxay jirtaa . . . kiiloomitir?**
How far is the next village?	**Intee bay jirtaa tuuladan, tuulada ku xigtaa?**
Where can I find this address?	**Halkee ayaan cinwaankan ka helayaa?**
Can you show me (on the map)?	**Maabka ma iga tusi kartaa?**
How do I get to . . . ?	**Sideen ku tegi karaa . . . ?**
I want to go to . . .	**Waxaan doonayaa inaan tago . . .**
Can I walk there?	**Halkaa ma u lugayn karaa?**
Is it far?	**Miyay fogtahay?**
Is it near?	**Miyay dhawdahay?**
Is it far from/near here?	**Halkan miyay ka fogtahay/ dhawdahay?**
It is not far.	**Ma foga.**
Go straight ahead.	**Saani u soco.**
Turn left.	**Bidix u leexo.**
Turn right.	**Midig u leexo.**
at the next corner	**waa koonaha/rukunka kan xiga xaggiise**
at the traffic lights	**waa nalalka taraafiga xaggooda**

DIRECTIONS

behind	**xagga dambe/dabada**
far	**fog**
in front of	**hortiisa**
left	**bidix**
near	**dhaw**
opposite	**ka soo horjeeda**
right	**midig**
straight on	**toos; saani**

bridge	**buundo; biriish**
corner	**rukun; koone**
crossroads	**isgoysyo**
one-way street	**jid dhinac qudha loo maro**

north	**woqooyi**
south	**koonfur**
east	**bari**
west	**galbeed**

10. SHOPPING

Where can I find a . . . ?	**Xaggee ayaan ka heli karaa . . . ?**
Where can I buy . . . ?	**Xaggee ayaan ka iibsan karaa . . . ?**
Where's the market?	**Waa xaggee suuqu?**
Where's the nearest . . . ?	**Waa xaggee . . . ugu dhow?**
Can you help me?	**Ma i caawin kartaa?**
Can I help you?	**Ma ku caawin karaa?**
I'm just looking.	**Waan eegeegayaa uun.**
I'd like to buy . . .	**Waxa aan rabaa inaan soo iibsado . . .**
Could you show me some . . . ?	**Ma i tusi kartaa . . . ?**
Can I look at it?	**Ma eegi karaa?**
Do you have any . . . ?	**Waxba . . . ma ka haysaa?**
This.	**Kan.**
That.	**Kaas.**
I don't like it.	**Ma jecli.**
I like it.	**Waan jecelahay.**
Do you have anything cheaper?	**Midkale oo ka jaban/ raqiisaysaa ma haysaa?**
cheaper/better	**ka raqiisan/ka fiican**
larger/smaller	**ka weyn/ka yar**
Do you have anything else?	**Wax kale oo aan kan ahayn ma haysaa?**
Do you have any others?	**Kuwo kale ma haysaa?**
Sorry, this is the only one.	**Iga raalli ahow, kanoo kaliya baan hayaaye.**
I'll take it.	**Waan qaadan doonaa/ qaadanayaa.**
How much/many do you want?	**Waa immisa/meeqa qiimahaad rabtaa?**

How much is this?	**Waa immisa kanu/tanu?***
Can you write down the price?	**Qiimaha ma qori kartaa?**
Could you lower the price?	**Qiimaha ma jebin kartaa?**
I don't have much money.	**Lacag badan ma haysto.**
Do you take credit cards?	**Kiridit kaadhka ma qaadataa?**
Would you like it wrapped?	**Ma rabtaa inaan duubiyo sida hay'ad oo kale.**
Will that be all?	**Wax kale ma rabtaa?**
Thank you, goodbye.	**Mahadsanid, nabadgelyo.**
I want to return this.	**Waxa aan rabaa kan inaan celiyo.**

USEFUL WORDS

auto spares store	**bakhaarka isbeerbaadhka baabuurta?**
baker's	**moofada**
bank	**bangi**
barber's	**timojare**
I want a haircut please.	**Fadlan timaha in la ii jaro ayaan doonayaa.**
bookshop	**dukaan buugagga**
butcher's	**hilible**
pharmacy	**farmasii**
clothes store	**bacadle dharka**
dentist	**dhakhtarka ilkaha**
department store	**dukaan aad u weyn**
dressmaker	**dawaarle; harqaan**
electrical goods store	**dukaanka qalabka laydhtiriigga**
florist	**dukaanka ubaxyada iibiya/gada**
greengrocer	**booshari**
hairdresser	**timoqurxiye**

* **kanu** for a masculine thing, **tanu** for a feminine thing.

hardware store	**bakaar alaabta dhismaha**
hospital	**casbitaal**
kiosk	**dabakaayo**
laundry	**doobi**
market	**suuq**
newsstand	**dabakaayo jaraa'id laga gado**
shoeshop	**dukaanka kabaha**
shop	**dukaan**
stationer's	**dukaan laga gado qalabka xafiiska**
supermarket	**subarmaarkad; baqaalad**
travel agent	**xafiiska tigidhada googa**
vegetable shop	**khudradle**
watchmaker's	**saacadoole**

CRAFTS & JEWELRY

Carved wooden combs are used by both sexes and are worn as ornaments in the hair. Women traditionally wear their hair long and display a dazzling range of coiffure styles. Ornaments are popular and those who can afford it prefer Arab-style jewelry, usually crafted in the towns on the coast. Necklaces are very striking and are made from pearls, leather, amber beads, silver and cowries. Women wear bracelets around their wrists, elbows and ankles, and are made of zinc, although rich women possess finely wrought bracelets of silver. Men wear necklaces or bracelets as talismans, often with a small leather pouch containing a fragment of the Qur'an. Wooden rosaries (**tusbax**) are also worn by religious people. Traditionally, warriors wore bracelets of ivory bracelets as a sign of their prowess in battle.

box	**sanduuq**
bracelet	**jijin̠**
carpet	**kaarbad**
chain	**silsilad**
clock	**saacad**
copper	**maar**
crystal	**wiriq**

earrings	**wasaaqyo**
enamel	**dheeh**
gold	**dahab**
handicraft	**farsamada gacanta**
iron	**bir; xadiid**
jade	**dhagax cagaaran**
jewelry	**dahab**
leather	**leedar; maas**
metal	**bir**
modern	**cusub; casri ah**
necklace	**silsilad luquuta lagu xirto**
pottery	**waxyaabo dhoobaha laga sameeyey**
ring	**kaatun**
rug	**sajaayad**
rosary	**tusbax**
silver	**silfar; naxaas**
steel	**bir; xadiid**
stone	**dhagax**
traditional	**qalab dhaqan; hidde ah**
vase	**weel**
watch	**saacad**
wood	**qori**

TOILETRIES

aspirin	**asbiriin**
bandaid	**bandeej**
comb	**shanlo**
condom	**kondham**
cotton wool	**cudbi**
deodorant	**shiirdhawr**
hairbrush	**baraashka timaha**
lipstick	**xammuurad**
mascara	**waxay dumarka baalashooda marsadaan**
mouthwash	**luqluq**

nail clippers	**qalabka ciddi lagu jaro**
painkillers	**xanuun joojiye**
perfume	**udgoon**
powder	**budo**
razor	**sakiin**
razorblade	**sakiin**
shampoo	**shaanboo**
shaving cream	**saabuunta gadh xiirashada**
sleeping pills	**kiniinka hurdada**
soap	**saabuun**
sponge	**isbuunyo**
tampons	**tambooni**
thermometer	**heerkul beeg**
tissues	**sooft beebar; kiliinikis; tishiyuu**
toilet paper	**tooylad beebar**
toothbrush	**caday burush ah**
toothpaste	**dawada cadayga**

CLOTHES

Somali traditional clothing is notable for its use of cotton (**suuf**). The loose gowns worn by both men and women is the **maro** or **toob**. Men may wear a white or colored loincloth and either a full **maro** or a half **maro**, which covers their shoulders. These are naturally white or grey, or can be dyed red or yellow. The robes worn by women are more varied and vary according to their status or position in life. Women closely linked to the Sufi orders would wear colored jackets and stockings. Men sometimes would wear a dagger (**toorri**), which is strapped to the waist by a leather belt.

bag	**shandad**
belt	**suun**
boots	**buudh**
cotton	**cudbi**
dress	**direys; dhar**
gloves	**galoofyo**
handbag	**shandad gacmeed**

hat	**koofiyad**
jacket	**jaakeet**
jeans	**jiinis**
leather	**liidar; harag**
overcoat	**oborkoodh**
pocket	**jeeb**
scarf	**iskaaf**
shirt	**shaadh**
shoes	**kabo**
socks	**sharabaaddo**
suit	**suudh**
sweater	**funaanad**
tie	**niigteyn**
trousers	**surwaal**
umbrella	**dallaayad**
underwear	**hoos gashi**
uniform	**direys**
wool	**suuf**

STATIONERY

ballpoint	**bolboynit**
dictionary	**dhigshaneeri; qaamuus**
envelope	**gal**
guidebook	**tilmaansiiye**
ink	**khad**
magazine	**jaariidad; wargeys**
map	**maab; khariidad**
road map	**maabka waddooyinka**
a map of Mogdishu	**Moqdishu* maabkeeda; maabka Moqdishu**
newspaper	**jariidad**
a newspaper in English	**jariidad Ingriisi ah**
notebook	**xusuusqor**
novels in English	**noofallo Af Ingriisi ah**

* Often referred to as **Xamar** (the name for the old centre of the city).

(piece of) paper	**xaashi; warqad; waraaq**
pen	**qalin; ben**
pencil	**qalin; beensal; qori; laabbis**
postcard	**booskaadh**
scissors	**maqas**
writing paper	**warqad/xaashida wax lagu qoro**
Do you have any foreign publications?	**Ma haysaa wax qoraalo kutub ah oo ajanebi ah?**

PHOTOGRAPHY

How much is it to process this film?	**Safaynta filimkani immasa ayuu qiimihiisu noqonayaa?**
When will it be ready?	**Goorma ayaad diyaarin kartaa?**
I'd like a film for this camera.	**Kamaradan ayaan filim u rabaa?**

camera	**kamara**
color (film)	**filim kalar leh; filim midab leh**
film	**filim**
flash	**falaash**
lens	**bikaaco**
light meter	**iftiinbeege**

SMOKING

A packet of cigarettes, please.	**Fadlan baakidh sigaar ah.**
Are these cigarettes strong/mild?	**Sigaaradassi ma qaar culus/ fudud baa?**
Do you have a light?	**Wallaacad ma haysaa?**
Do you have any American cigarettes?	**Wax sigaar maraykan ah ma haysaa?**

cigar	**sigaar**
cigarette papers	**waraaqaha sigaarka**

SHOPPING

cigarettes	**sigaar**
a carton of cigarettes	**kartoon sigaar ah**
filtered	**buush leh**
filterless	**bilaa buush ah**
flint	**dhagax bilikeega lagu isticmaalaa**
lighter fluid	**gaasta bilikeega**
lighter	**bilikee**
matches	**kabriid; qaraf; taraq**
pipe	**beeb**
tobacco	**buuri; tubaako**

ELECTRICAL APPLIANCES

adapter	**bareesada korontada qaybisa**
battery	**batari**
cd	**sii-dii**
cd player	**sii-dii rakoodh**
fan	**marwaxad**
hairdryer	**heerdarayer**
iron (for clothing)	**kaawiyad**
kettle	**kildhi**
plug	**balaag**
portable tv	**tii-vii la qaadi karaa**
radio	**raadiyow**
record	**rikoodh**
tape (cassette)	**cajalad**
tape recorder	**rikoodh**
television	**telefishan**
transformer	**korontooge**
video (player)	**fiidiyow**
videotape	**cajalad fiidiyow**
voltage regulator	**korontosime**

SIZES

small	**yar**
big	**weyn**

heavy	**culus**
light	**fudud**
more	**ka badan**
less	**ka yar**
too much/many	**aad u badan**
many	**badan**
enough	**ku filan**
that's enough	**intaas baa ku fulan**
also	**sidoo kale**
a little bit	**in yar**

Do you have a carrier bag? **Bac miyaad haysaa?**

> **NOTE ON 'VERY'** – **Aad + u** is used to express 'very,' e.g.
> <u>**Aad**</u> **baan** <u>**u**</u> **fiicanahay.** 'I am very well.'

11. WHAT'S TO SEE

Do you have a guide-book/local map?
Miyaad haysaa buug ah maabka degaankan?

Is there a guide who speaks English?
Qof wax hagi karaa oo Af Ingiriisiga ku hadlaa halkan ma joogaa?

What are the main attractions?
Meelihii soo jiidasho leh maxay yihiin?

What is that?
Kaasi muxuu yahay?

How old is it?
Waa immisa jir?

May I take a photograph?
Ma sawiri karaa?

What time does it open/close?
Immisadaa la furaa/la xidhaa?

What is this monument?
Taalladii waa maxay?

What does that say?
Kaasi muxuu leeyahay?

Who is that statue of?
Taalladii yay matalaysaa?

Is there an entrance fee?
Gelitaanka meesha wax lacag ah miyaa layska rabaa?

How much?
Waa intee?

Are there any night clubs?
Ma jiraan goleyaa caways?

Where can I hear local folk music?
Xaggeen ka dhegaysan karaa muusig hidde ah?

How much does it cost to get in?
Immisaa halkaas lagu bixiyaa?

What's there to do in the evenings?
Halkan cawaysyada maxaa la sameeyaa?

Is there a concert?
Riwaayad ma jirtaa?

When is the wedding?
Aroosku waa goorma?

What time does it begin?
Goorma ayuu bilaabmayaa?

Can we swim here?	**Halkan ma ku dabbaalan karnaa?**
dancing	**qoobka ciyaar**
disco	**disko**
exhibition	**bandhig**
traditional dancing	**faalkaloor/ciyaaro hiddood**
traditional music	**muusig hidde ah**
jazz	**jaas**
party	**baadhi**
rock 'n' roll	**rok-aan-rool**
blues	**buluus**

BUILDINGS

academy	**akadeemi**
apartment	**guri dabakh ah**
archeological	**qadiimi ah**
art gallery	**rugta bandhigga farshaxanka**
bakery	**moofo; foorno**
bar	**bar; maqaahi**
apartment block	**dhismo dabakh ah**
building	**dhisme**
casino	**kaasiino**
castle	**qalcad**
cemetery	**xabaalo**
church	**kiniisad**
cinema	**sinimoo**
city-map	**maabka magaalada**
college	**koolaj**
concert hall	**guriga riwaayadaha**
concert	**riwaayad**
elevator	**wiish**
embassy	**safaarad**
hospital	**cusbitaal**
house	**guri**

housing project	**mashruuca guriyaynta**
library	**ragta kutabta; laabareeri**
madrasa	**madrasa**
main square	**gooladda muhiimka ah**
market	**suuq**
monument	**faallo**
mosque	**masaajid**
museum	**guriga carwada**
nightclub	**naayt kilaab**
old city	**magaalada qadiimi ah**
park	**beer**
parliament building	**dhismaha baarlamaanka**
restaurant	**maqaahi; hudheel**
saint's tomb	**maqaam**
school	**dugsi; iskuul**
shop	**dukaan; daas; macdaar**
shrine	**meel caabudaad loo aado**
stadium	**istaadiyam**
statue	**faallo**
synagogue	**macbadka yuhuudda**
theatre	**tiyaatar**
tomb	**xabaal**
tower	**faallo**
university	**jaamacad**
zoo	**beerta xayawaanka**

OCCASIONS

birth	**dhalasho**
death	**dhimasho**
funeral	**aas**
marriage	**guur**

SOCIAL TIES

FAMILY — Somalis have an extremely sophisticated way of defining the different groups of family and degrees of relationship, due in part to the clan system and the fact that men can have more than one wife under Islamic law. For example, the single English word 'family' is translated as **bah** or **xaas** when it refers to the 'mother and her children,' **xaasas** when it means the 'wife/wives and children of one man,' **qoys** when it refers to the 'general immediate family,' and **reer** is a very flexible group word which can describe the 'extended family.'

Xiddid — 'family ties,' referring to the relationship established by marriage — are an important force in Somali society and these form the bedrock of **xeerka qoyska** 'family law.' Families and clans alike look to their **odayaal** — 'elders' or 'wisemen' — for guidance. **Duq** or **akhyaar** — terms also heard to describe an elder — can also be used for anyone you respect, and are often heard on the radio when broadcasters are referring to the listeners.

CLANS — Perhaps the dominant form of social organization in Somali society is the clan system. Clan ties are based on kinship more than region, and all Somali ethnic groups have a common cultural background, but there is still a great difference between the pastoral Samaale groups — the Dir, Isaq, Hawiya and Darod clans — and the Southern, sedentary Sab peoples — including the Digil and Rahanwein.

Certain clans (**qabiil**) have heads who may be called **ugaas**, **suldhaan** or **garaad**. **Tol** is the word used to express the concept of 'clan descent or genealogy.'

12. FINANCE

Currencies — The official currency in Somalia is the **shilin**, divided into 100 **senti**. Unofficially in use, but still accepted everywhere outside of government establishments and official retail outlets, are U.S. dollars. These may be refused however if notes are creased, torn, old, or simply a low denomination. Be prepared to accept change in Somali currency.

Changing money — In the absence of a reliable banking system, money is best changed in any bureau de change, where you will find reliable, up-to-date exchange rates prominently displayed on a board. The cashiers will often know a European language or two, and almost all will show the workings of the exchange on a calculator for you. Many shops and stalls will also be happy to change money for you.

Where can I change some money?	**Xaggeen ka sarifan karaa xoogaa lacag ah?**
I want to change some dollars.	**Waxaan rabaa xoogaa doolar ah inaan sarifto.**
I want to change some pounds.	**Waxaan rabaa xoogaa giniya ah inaan sarifto.**
What is the exchange rate?	**Qiimaha sarifku waa intee?**
What is the commission?	**Immisaa dilaal ah?**
Could you please check that again?	**Fadlan mar labaad ma ii hubin kartaa?**
Do you have a calculator?	**Kalkulaytar ma leedahay?**

dollar	**doolar**
franc	**faran**
mark	**maark**
shilling	**shilin**
sterling	**istaraliini**

bank notes	**jeegag**
calculator	**kaalkulaytar**
cashier	**xisaabiye**
coins	**qadaadiic**
credit card	**kiridhiid kaadh**
commission	**dilaalis; mashqaayad**
exchange	**sarif**
(loose) change	**baaqi**
signature	**saxeex**

A NOTE ON RELIGIOUS HERITAGE

Sufism — Many Somalis were traditionally associated with Sufi **tariiqas** (sects or 'paths'), followers of the mystical side of Islam. There are three **tariiqas** — the Qadiriya, the Ahmadiya and the Salihiya. Few Somalis actively participate in the religious side of this, while these sects transcend clan groupings (see page 127).

The sheikhs or leaders (**wadaad**) of the sects act as widely regarded community leaders or spokesmen. Since the beginning of Islam many sheikhs have become saints and their tombs are important sources of pilgrimage and holy places. Some of these are clan ancestors, while others are revered for their religious powers.

Holidays & festivals — There are a wide variety of traditional festivals celebrated in every area. Important dates in the national calendar include **Ramadhaan** (Ramadan) and **Ciidda Carrafo** (also known as simply **Ciid**). A popular festival is the **Mawliid**, originating from a celebration in verse and song of the Prophet Muhammad's birthday, and now used as a vibrant means of celbrating events of significance to the community.

13. COMMUNICATIONS

Telecommunications — Facilities should be available from towns and cities to make international calls.

AT THE POST OFFICE

Where is the post office?	**Waa xaggee boostadu?**
What time does the post office open?	**Wakhtigee baa boosta la furaa?**
What time does the post office close?	**Wakhtigee baa boosta la xidhaa?**
Where is the mail box?	**Mee sanduuqii waraaqu?**
Is there any mail for me?	**Wax waraaqo ahi ma ii yaalaan?**
How long will it take for this to get there?	**Intee ayay qaadanaysaa inay halkaas gaadho?**
How much does it cost to send this to . . . ?	**Immisa ayuu qiimahii yahay warqadan in loo diro . . . ?**
I would like some stamps.	**Waxaan doonayaa tigidho.**
I would like to send . . .	**Waxaan doonayaa inaan diro . . .**
a letter	**warqad**
a postcard	**booskaadh**
a parcel	**baarsal**
a telegram	**teligraam; taar**
air mail	**warqad hawada loo diro**
envelope	**gal**
mailbox	**sanduuqa waraaqaha**
parcel	**baarsal**
registered mail	**warqad rajistar ah**
stamp	**tigidh**

TELEPHONING

Where is the telephone?	**Waa xaggee teliitoonku.**
May I use your phone?	**Tilifoonkaaga ma isticmaali karaa?**
Can I telephone from here?	**Halkan tilifoonka ma ka diri karaa?**
Can you help me get this number?	**Ma i caawin kartaa inaan helo lambarkan?**
I would like to make a phone call.	**Waxaan rabaa inaan tilifoon diro?**
I would like to send a fax.	**Waxaan rabaa inaan faagas diro.**
I would like to send a telex.	**Waxaan rabaa inaan teleges diro.**
I want to ring . . .	**Waxaan rabaa inaan tilifoon diro . . .**
What is the code for . . . ?	**Waa immisa furaha . . . lagu galaa?**
What is the international code?	**Waa immisa furaha caalamiga ahi?**
The number is . . .	**Lamabarku waa . . .**
The extension is . . .	**Ekestanshanku waa . . .**
It's busy.	**Waa mashquul.**
I've been cut off.	**Wuu iga go'ay.**
The lines have been cut.	**Khadadkani way go'anyihiin.**
Can you help me get this number?	**Inaan lambarkan helo ma igu caawin kartaa?**
Can I dial direct?	**Waa xaggee tilifoon dadweynuhu isticmaali karo ka ugu dhawi?**
Where is the nearest public phone?	**Waa xagee tilifoon bablig ah ka ugu dhawi?**

I would like to speak to . . .	**Waxaan doonayaa inaan la hadlo . . .**
Can I leave a message?	**Farriin ma u dhaafi karaa?**
fax	**faagas**
e-mail	**waraaq e-mayl ah**
international operator	**obraytar caalamka ah/ dibada**
Internet	**Internet**
modem	**moodem**
operator	**obraytar; xiriiriye telefoon**
satellite phone	**dayaxgacmeedka tilifoonada**
telex	**telegas**

COURTESY

There is a special form, the vocative, which is used when speaking to people: **-ay** is added to female names and **-ow** to male names, e.g.

Faadum<u>ay</u>! Faadumo!   **Maxamed<u>ow</u>!** Maxamed!

14. THE OFFICE

chair	**kursi**
computer	**kumbuyuutar**
desk	**deski**
drawer	**khaanad**
fax	**faagas**
file	**fayl**
meeting	**shir**
paper	**warqad**
pen	**qalin; ben**
pencil	**qalin beensal; qalin qori**
photocopier	**footo koobi**
printer	**birintar**
report	**warbixin**
ruler	**masdarad**
telephone	**tilifoon**
telex	**teleges**
typewriter	**teeb**

15. THE CONFERENCE

conference room	**qolka shirka**
copy	**koobi**
discussion	**wadahadal**
guest speaker	**jeediye la martiqaaday**
a paper	**warqad**
podium	**mimbar**
projector	**baroojektar**
speaker	**qofkii khudbaneynaya**
subject	**mawduuc**

16. THE FARM

agriculture	cilmiga beeraha
barn	bakaar weyn
cattle	lo'
to clear land	dhul bannee
corn	galley
crops	midho
earth	dhul
fallowland	dhul aan la beerin
farm	beer
farmer	beeraley
farming	beerasho
animal feed	xoolo daajin
fertilizer	nafaqeeye
field	beer; garoon
fruit	khudrad
garden	beer
to grow crops	wax beer
harvest	goosasho
hay	caws engegsan
haystack	raso caws engegsan
marsh	meel dhul qoyan leh
mill	rugta wax lagu shiido
orchard	goob dhirta midhaha laga rifo
planting	beerid
plow	makiinadda carro rogidda
to plow	carro rog
reaping	gurro
season	xilli
seed	siidh; iniin
sowing	abuur
tractor	cagafcagaf
wheat	sarreen
well (of water)	ceel

17. ANIMALS

bull	**dibi**
camel	**hal; awr**
camels	**geel**
cat	**bisad; dinnad; mukulaal**
cow	**sac**
dog	**ey**
donkey	**dameer**
elephant	**maroodi**
gazelle	**deero; golcas**
goat	**ri**
herd of camels	**kadin**
herd of horses	**raxan**
horse	**faras**
lamb	**nayl**
lion	**libaax**
mare	**geenyo**
mouse	**jiir**
mule	**baqal**
pig	**doofaar**
pony	**faras yar**
rabbit	**bakayle**
ram	**wan**
rat	**jiir**
sheep	**ido**
stallion	**faras lab ah**
wild dog	**yey**

BIRDS

bird	**shimbir**
bird of prey	**haad**
chicken/hen	**digaag; digaagad; dooro**
guinea fowl	**digiiran**
hawk	**dhuuryo**
crow	**tuke**

duck	**boolonboollo**
eagle	**gorgor**
ostrich	**goroyo**
owl	**guumays**
rooster	**diiq**
turkey	**turki**
vulture	**gorgor**

INSECTS & AMPHIBIANS

ant	**qudhaanjo**
bee	**shinni**
butterfly	**balanbaalis**
caterpillar	**dirindiir**
cockroach	**baranbaro**
dung beetle	**xaar walwaal**
fish	**kalluun**
flea	**dhuudhi**
fly	**duqsi**
frog	**rah**
insect	**cayayaan**
lizard	**qorrato; qallajis**
louse	**injir**
mosquito	**kaneeco**
scorpion	**dibqallooc**
snail	**xaaxeeyo**
snake	**mas**
spider	**caaro**
termite	**aboor**
tick	**shilin**
wasp	**laxle**
worm	**dirixi**

18. COUNTRYSIDE

canal	**biyomareen**
cave	**god**
dam	**dhaam; biyoxidh**
earthquake	**dhulgariir**
fire	**dab**
flood	**daad**
foothpath	**waddo lugeed; wadiiqo**
forest	**kayn**
hill	**gunbur**
lake	**haro**
mountain	**buur**
plain	**meel siman**
plant	**geed**
river bank	**daafta webiga**
river	**webi**
rock	**dhadhaab**
slope	**tiiro**
stream	**durdur**
tree	**geed**
valley	**dooxo**
waterfall	**biyo dhac**
a wood	**duur**

THE NOMADIC LIFE

Traditionally a pastoralist society — a way of life still vital to a large section of the population of Somalia — Somalis have many special words for their grazing animals and the nomadic life that goes with tending them. Apart from the words for individual types of animals there are special words for groups of animals, e.g. **adhi** 'sheep & goats' and **geel** 'camels'. Social words include **guri** 'nomadic domestic group,' while nomads are called **reer guura** 'migrating people.' Their grazing encampments are called **degmooyin** (*singular* **degmo**). People living along and between the two main rivers Webi Jubba and Webi Shabeelle (see next section) practise agriculture.

19. THE WEATHER

Much of Somalia is covered by often impenetrable flat plateaus and plains covered with scrub bush. The northern coastal plains are particularly arid — they are called **guban** or 'burned' because of their scorched appearance. Inland are the Oggo Highlands which turn to low-lying hills and valleys with rivers, but only two — the Jubba and Webi Shabeelle in the south — contain water all year round. This is where most of the country's agriculture is centred .

The Somali year is divided into four seasons which are defined by rainfall or lack of it:

Jiilaal (December-March) is the hot, dry season when the north-east tradewind or **jiilaashin** blows.

Gu' (April-June) is the main wet season, with heavy rains.

Xagaa (July-August) is mainly a dry season when the south-west tradewind or **xagaashin** blows, with some rain falling in the south.

Dayr (September-November) is the lesser wet season, with light rains.

Rainfall averages annually at less than 17 inches in most areas. The climate is tropical, with little seasonal change in temperature across most of the country. While the mean temperature is 24-31°C, the interior and area on the Gulf of Aden are hotter and the plateaus cooler.

What's the weather like?	**Cimiladu maanta waa sidee?**
The weather is . . . today.	**Cimiladu maanta waa . . .**
cold	**qabow; dhaxan**
cool/fresh	**iska dhaxan**
cloudy	**mid daruuro leh**
foggy	**ceeryaamo**
freezing	**baraf**
hot	**kulayl**
very hot	**aad bay u kulushey**
windy	**dabayl leh**
It is raining.	**Roob baa da'aya.**
It is snowing.	**Baraf baa dhacaya.**
It is sunny.	**Cadceed baa jirta.**

air	**hawo**
cloud	**daruur**
drought	**abaar**
duststorm	**siigo**
famine	**cunto la'aan**
sea fog	**ceeryaamo xagga badda**
frost	**dhedo**
full moon	**shaniyo tobnaad; dayax dhamays ah**
ice	**baraf**
midsummer	**badhtamaha xagaaga**
midwinter	**badhtamaha jiilaalka**
mild winter	**jiilaal aan sidaas u xumayn**
moon	**dayax**
new moon	**bil**
parched earth	**dhul qallalan**
rain	**roob**
sleet	**roob barafle ah**
snow	**baraf**
star	**xiddig**
sun	**cadceed; qorrax**
sunny	**cadceed baa jirta**
weather	**cimilo**
wind	**dabayl**

20. CAMPING

Where can we camp?	**Halkee baynu degi karraa?**
Can we camp here?	**Halkan ma degi karraa?**
Is it safe to camp here?	**Ammaan ma tahay halkani haddii aynu degno?**
Is there drinking water?	**Halkani biyo ma leedahay?**
May we light a fire?	**Dab miyaan shidi karraa?**
ax	**faash**
backpack	**boorso dhabarka lagu qaato**
bucket	**baaldi**
campsite	**meel teendhooyin lagu dhisi karaa**
can opener	**manfag**
compass	**jiheeye**
firewood	**xaabo**
flashlight	**falaashlaydh**
hammer	**dubbe**
lamp	**laambad; nal**
mattress	**joodari**
penknife	**mindi laysku laabo**
rope	**xadhig**
sleeping bag	**isliibin baag**
stove	**furinyar**
tent	**taanbuug; teendho**
tent pegs	**biro feendho**
water bottle	**quraarad biyood**

21. IN CASE OF EMERGENCY

Complaining — If you really feel you have been cheated or misled, raise the matter first with your host or the proprietor of the establishment in question — preferably with a smile. Somalis are proud but courteous and they consider it their duty to help any guest. Angry glares and shouting will get you nowhere.

Crime — Somalis are law-abiding people, but petty theft does occur. Without undue paranoia, take usual precautions: watch your wallet or purse, securely lock your equipment and baggage before handing it over to railway or airline porters, and don't leave valuables on display in your hotel room. If you are robbed, contact the police. Of course, in the more remote areas, sensible precautions should be taken and always ensure that you go with a guide. In general, follow the same rules as you would in your own country and you will run little risk of encountering crime.

What to do if you lose something — Save time and energy by appealing only to senior members of staff or officials. If you have lost items in the street or left anything in public transport, the police may be able to help.

Disabled facilities — The terrain and conditions throughout most of Somalia do not make it easy for any visitor to get around in a wheelchair even at the best of times. Access to most buildings in cities and towns is difficult, particularly since the majority of lifts function irregularly. Facilities are rarely available in hotels, airports or other public areas.

Toilets — You will find public utilities located in any important or official building. You may use those in hotels or restaurants. You may often encounter failed plumbing and absence of toilet paper.

Help!	**Hayaay!**
Could you help me please?	**Fadlan ma i caawin kartaa?**
Do you have a telephone?	**Tilifoon ma haysataa?**
Can I use your telephone?	**Tilifoonkaaga ma isticmaali karaa?**
Where is the nearest telephone?	**Waa xaggee tilifoonka halkan ugu dhowi?**
Does the phone work?	**Tilifoonkani ma shaqaynayaa?**

Get help quickly!	**Si degdeg ah kaalmo u hel!**
Call the police.	**Booliiska u yeedh/wac**
I'll call the police!	**Booliiskaan u yeedhayaa/ wacayaa!**
Is there a doctor near here?	**Dhakhtar halkan ma ka dhawyey?**
Call the doctor!	**Dhakhtarka u yeedh!**
Call the ambulance!	**Ambalaaska u yeedh!**
I'll get medical help!	**Waxaan heli doonaa kaalmo caafimaad!**
Where is the doctor?	**Mee dhakhtarku?*/ Mee dhakhtaraddu?****
Where is the hospital?	**Waa xaggee cusbitaalku?**
Where is the chemist?	**Farmasigu waa xaggee?**
Where is the dentist?	**Dhakahtarka ilkuhu waa xaggee?**
Where is the police station?	**Isteeshinka bilaysku waa xaggee?**
There's been an accident!	**Shil baa dhacay.**
Is anyone hurt?	**Qofna wax ma ku noqday?**
This person is hurt.	**Qofkan baa wax ku noqday.**
There are people injured.	**Dadkan baa ku dhaawacmay.**
Don't move!	**Ha dhaqaaqin!**
Go away!	**Soco/tag/fogoow**
I am lost.	**Waan lunsan ahay.**
I am ill.	**Waan bukaa/ xanuunsanayaa.**
I've been raped.	**Waa lay kufsaday.**
Take me to the doctor.	**Dhakhtarka i gee.**
I've been robbed.	**Waa lay dhacay/waan dhacanahay.**
Thief!	**Tuug!**
My . . . has been stolen.	**. . . waa layga xaday.**
I have lost my . . .	**Waxa iga lumay . . .**
my bags	**shandadahaygu**
my camera equipment	**qalabkii kamaradayada**

* male doctor ** female doctor

my handbag	**shandadaydii gacanta**
my laptop computer	**kombutarkaygii laabtobka ahaa**
my money	**lacagtaydii**
my passport	**baasaboorkaygii**
my travelers' checks	**jeegagaygii ahaa kuwa wareega**
my wallet	**shandadaydii jeebka**

My possessions are insured.	**Alaabadaydu caymis bay ku jirtaa.**
I have a problem.	**Dhibaataan haystaa.**
I didn't do it.	**Sidaas maan samaynin.**
I'm sorry.	**Waan ka xumahay.**
I apologize.	**Waan ka xumahay.**
I didn't realize anything was wrong.	**Maan rumaysnayn in wax khalad ahi arrintaas ku jiray.**
I want to contact my embassy.	**Waxaan doonayaa inaan la xidhiidho safaaradayda.**
I want to contact my consulate.	**Waxaan rabaa inaan la xidhiidho qunsaliyaddayda.**
I speak English.	**Af Ingiriisiga baan ku hadlaa.**
I need an interpreter.	**Turjubaan baan u baahanahay.**
Where are the toilets?	**Meeye suuliyadu/ baytalmaygu.**

clinic	**kiliinik**
doctor	**dhakhtar;* dhakhtarad****
nurse	**kalkaaliye; kalkaaliso; neeras**
hospital	**cusbitaal**
policeman	**bilays; booliis**
police	**bilays; booliis**
police station	**isteeshin bilays/booliis**

* male doctor   ** female doctor

22. HEALTHCARE

Health/medical information — Make sure any insurance policy you take out covers Somalia, although this will only help in flying you out in case of a serious accident or illness. Vaccinations are required for Somalia — check with your doctor, who may also suggest you take other boosters usually recommended when making any trip outside of North America and Western Europe.

Pharmacies are not always easy to find and can be understocked. If planning to travel off the beaten track, it is probably best to bring a sufficient supply of any medication you require — even basics such as aspirin, cotton wool or sunburn lotion.

What's the trouble?	**Maxay tahay mushkiladu/ dhibaatadu?**
I am sick.	**Waan xanuunsanayaa.**
My companion is sick.	**Rafiiqaygii ayaa xanuunsanaya.**
May I see a female doctor?	**Ma arki karaa dhakhtarad naag ah?**
I have medical insurance.	**Waxaan ku jiraa caymis caafimaad.**
Please undress.	**Fadlan dharka iska bixi.**

AILMENTS

How long have you had this problem?	**Muddo intee le'eg baad dhibaatadan qabtay?**
How long have you been feeling sick?	**Muddo intee le'eg ayaad xanuunkan iska dareemaysay.**
Where does it hurt?	**Halkee ku xanuunaysa?**
It hurts here.	**Halkan bay i xanuunaysaa.**
I have been vomiting.	**Waan hunqaacayaa?**
I feel dizzy.	**Dawakhaad baan dareemayaa.**
I can't eat.	**Wax ma cuni karo.**
I can't sleep.	**Ma seexan karo.**

I feel worse.	**Waan ka sii darayaa.**
I feel better.	**Waan ka soo raynayaa.**
I am . . .	**Waxan qabaa . . .**
Are you . . . ?	**Miyaad qabtaa . . . ?**
diabetic	**kaadi sonkor**
epileptic	**sarco**
asthmatic	**xiiq**

I'm pregnant.	**Uur baan leeyahay.**

I have . . .	**Waxaan leeyahay . . .**
You have . . .	**Waxaad leedahay . . .**
a temperature	**xummad**
an allergy	**alerjig**
an infection	**caabuq**
an itch	**cuncun**
fever	**xummad**

I have a cold.	**Dhaxan baa igu dhacay.**
You have a cold.	**Duray baa kugu dhacay.**
I have a cough.	**Qufac baan leeyahay.**
You have a cough.	**Qufac baad leedahay.**

I have a headache.	**Madax xanuun baan leeyahay.**
I have toothache.	**Ilko xanuun baan leeyahay.**
I have a sore throat.	**Cuno xanuun baan leeyahay.**
I have a stomachache.	**Calool xanuun baan leeyahay.**
I have backache.	**Dhabar xanuun baan leeyahay.**
I have constipation.	**Calool istaag baan leeyahay.**
I have diarrhea.	**Shuban baan leeyahay.**

I have a heart condition.	**Wadne xanuun baan leeyahay.**
I have a pain in my heart.	**Wadnaha ayaa xumadi iga haysaa.**

MEDICATION

I take this medication.	**Dawadan waan qaataa.**
I need medication for . . .	**Waxaan u baahanahay dawada . . .**
What type of medication is this?	**Dawadani waa noocee?**
How many times a day must I take it?	**Immisa goor baan maalintii dawadan qaadan doonaa?**
When should I stop?	**Goormaan joojin doonaa?**
I'm on antibiotics.	**Antibayootiig baan qaataa.**
I'm allergic to antibiotics.	**Antibaayootiga elerjik baan ku ahay.**
I'm allergic to penicillin	**Beynasaliinta elerjik baan ku ahay.**
I have been vaccinated.	**Waa lay tallaalay.**
I have my own syringe.	**Anaa siliijkayga sita.**
Is it possible for me to travel?	**Inaan muddada dawadani ii socoto socdaal galaa suurtogal ma yahay?**
painkiller	**xanuun joojiye**
tranquilizer	**kiniin dejiye ah**
aspirin	**asbiriin**
antibiotic	**antibaayootig**
drug	**dawo**

HEALTH WORDS

AIDS	**eeydhis**
alcoholic	**khamriya cab**
alcoholism	**khamriya cabnimo; isbiirtoolenimo**
anemia	**dhiigla'aan**
amputation	**laf goyn**

anesthetic	**suuxiye**
anesthetist	**dhakhtarka suuxinta**
antibiotic	**antibaayootig**
antiseptic	**jeermisreeb**
blood	**dhiig**
blood group	**nooca dhiigga**
blood pressure:	**dhiig kac**
low blood pressure	**hoos u dhaca dhiigga**
high blood pressure	**dhiig kac**
blood transfusion	**dhiig ku shubid**
bone	**laf**
cancer	**kansar**
cholera	**daacuun**
clinic	**kiliinig**
dentist	**dhakhtarka ilkaha**
epidemic	**safmar**
fever	**xummad**
flu	**hargab**
fracture	**jabniin**
frostbite	**dhaawac qabowgu sababo**
germs	**jeermis**
heart attack	**wadne istaag**
hepatitis	**joonis**
hygiene	**nadiifnimo**
indigestion	**calool qushqush**
infection	**caabuq**
influenza	**hargab**
limb	**addin**
needle	**irbad**
nurse	**kalkaaliye**
operating theatre	**qolka qalliinka**
(surgical) operation	**qalliin**
oxygen	**ogsajiin**
pain	**xanuun**
pins & needles	**kabuubyo**
rabies	**reymis**

shrapnel	**firdhaad qarax**
snake bite	**qaniinyo mas**
stomachache	**calool xanuun**
surgeon	**dhakhtarka qalliinka**
(act of) surgery	**qallitaan**
syringe	**siliij**
thermometer	**heerkul beeg**
toothache	**ilig xanuun**
torture	**jidh dil**

EYESIGHT

I have broken my glasses.	**Muraayadii araga ayaa iga jabtay.**
Can you repair them?	**Ma ii hagaajin/samayn kartaa?**
I need new lenses.	**Muraayad cusub baan u baahanahay.**
When can I collect them?	**Goorma ayaan qaadan karaa?**
How much do I owe you?	**Immisa weeye qiimaha aad iga rabtaa?**

23. RELIEF AID

Can you help me?	**Ma i caawin kartaa?**
Do you speak English?	**Miyaad Af Ingriisiga ku hadashaa?**
Who is in charge?	**Halkan yaa xukuma?**
Fetch the main person in charge.	**Qofka u mudan keen.**
What's the name of this town?	**Magaaladan magaceed?**
How many people live there?	**Dad intee le'eg baa halkan ku nool?**
What's the name of that river?	**Webigaas magaciis?**
How deep is it?	**Intee ayuu dhererkiisu hoos u jiraa?**
Is the bridge still standing?	**Biriishki weli miyuu taaganyahay/dhisanyay?**
What is the name of that mountain?	**Buurtaas magaceed?**
How high is it?	**Dhererkeedu waa intee?**
Where is the border?	**Xuduuddu waa halkee/xaggee?**
Is it safe?	**Ammaan ma tahay?**
Show me.	**I tus.**

CHECKPOINTS

checkpoint	**kaantarool**
roadblock	**waddo xidhan**
Stop!	**Joogso!**
Do not move!	**Ha dhaqaaqin!**
Go!	**Tag/soco!**
Who are you?	**Kumaad*/Tumaad** tahay?**

* If 'you' is male.   ** If 'you' is female.

Don't shoot!	**Ha toogan!**
Help!	**Hayaay!**
no entry	**lama geli karo**
no admission	**ruqso ma laha**
emergency exit	**iridda bixidda xaalada degdeg ah**
straight on	**toos u soco**
turn left	**bidix u leexo**
turn right	**midig u leexo**
this way	**waddadan hay**
that way	**waddadaas hay**
Keep quiet!	**Is deji!**
You are right.	**Sax baad tahay.**
You are wrong.	**Waad khaldantahay.**
I am ready.	**Diyaar baan ahay.**
I am in a hurry.	**Waan degdegsanahay.**
Well, thank you! *(in reply)*	**Waa yahay, waad mahadsantay!**
What's that?	**Waa maxay waxaasi?**
Come in!	**Soo gal!; Soo dhowow!**
That's all!	**Waa arrin dhamaatay!**

FOOD DISTRIBUTION

This is a feeding station.	**Tani waa xarunta quudinta.**
How many people in your family?	**Qoyskaagu immisa qof buu ka koobanyahay?**
How many children?	**Immisaa caruur ah?**
You must come back this afternoon.	**Waa inaad kan la soo noqoto galabtan.**
tonight	**caawa**
tomorrow	**berrito**
the day after	**saa dambe**
next week	**todobaadka dambe**
There is water for you.	**Waa kuwan biyahaagii.**
There is grain for you.	**Waa kuwan midhahaagii.**
There is food for you.	**Cuntadan adigaa iska leh.**
There is fuel for you.	**Shidaalkan adigaa iska leh.**

ROAD REPAIR

Is the road passable?	**Waddadii ma la mari karaa?**
Are the bridges intact?	**Buundooyinka ma la mari karaa?**

Is the road blocked?	**Waddadii ma la xidhay?**
What is it blocked with?	**Muxuu yahay waxa xayiray?**
holes?	**godad?**
trees?	**dhir?**
rocks?	**dhadhaabo?**
something else?	**wax kale?**

Are there any road-building machines nearby?	**Makiinad waddooyin lagu dhiso meeshan u dhow ma jirtaa?**

We are repairing the road.	**Waddadan ayaan dib u hagaajinaynaa.**
We are repairing the bridge.	**Biriishkan ayaanu dib u hagaajinaynaa.**
We need . . .	**Waxaan u baahannahay . . .**
wood	**qoryo; looxaan**
rock	**dhadhaab**
gravel	**jay**
sand	**ciid**
fuel	**shidaal**

MINES

mine *noun*	**miino**
mines	**miinooyin**
minefield	**beermiino**
to lay mines	**miinooyin dhig; miinee**
to hit a mine	**miino jiidh**
to clear a mine	**miino saar**
mine detector	**qalab miinooyin lagu helo**
mine disposal	**miino gurid**

Are there any mines near here?	**Wax miino ah miyaa halkan ka dhaw?**
What type are they?	**Noocoodu waa maxay?**
anti-vehicle	**lidka gaadiidka?**
anti-personnel	**joogsi**
plastic	**raag**
floating	**biyood**
magnetic	**birlab ah**
tripwire	**jalfis**
What size are they?	**Intee bay le'egyihiin?**
What color are they?	**Midabkoodu waa maxay?**
Are they marked?	**Miyay calaamadsanyihiin?**
How?	**Sidee?**
How many mines are there?	**Immisa miino ah baa halkaas ku jiraa?**
When were they laid?	**Goormaa la dhigay?**
Can you take me to the minefield?	**Ma i geyn kartaa beerta miinada?**
Are they made from grenades, high explosives or something else?	**Ma waxay ka samaysanyihiin garnayl mise waxyaabaha qaraxa khatarta ah leh mise wax kale?**
Are they in a building?	**Ma dhismo ayay ku jiraan?**
on tracks?	**ma dariiqyo?**
on roads?	**ma waddo?**
on bridges?	**ma buundo?**
or elsewhere?	**mise meel kale?**
Can you show me?	**Ma i tusi kartaa?**

OTHER WORDS

airforce	**ciidanka cirka**
ambulance	**ambalaas**
armored car	**gaadhi ciidan**
army	**ciidan**
artillery	**madaafiicda goobta**
barbed wire	**gaabiyan**

bomb	**bambaane; bambo**
bomber	**duqeeye**
bullet	**xabbad**
cannon	**madfac culus**
disaster	**burbur**
fighter	**dagaalyahan**
gun	**qori**
machine gun	**boobe fudud**
missile	**gantaal**
missiles	**gantaallo**
natural disaster	**burbur dabiici**
navy	**ciidanka badda**
officer	**sarkaal**
parachute	**baarashuud**
peace	**nabad**
people	**dad**
pistol	**baastoolad**
refugee camp	**xero-qaxooti**
relief aid	**gargaar**
sack	**jawaan**
shell	**qashar**
shrapnel	**firdhaad qarax**
tank	**taangi; dubaabad**
troops	**ciidamo**
unexploded bomb	**bam aan qarxin**
United Nations	**Qaramada Midoobay**
war	**dagaal**

24. TOOLS

binoculars	**diirad**
brick	**bulukeeti**
brush	**burush**
cable	**silig**
cooker	**kuukar; cuntokariye**
drill	**dalooliye; diriil**
glasses, sunglasses	**muraayado**
hammer	**dubbe**
handle	**siddo**
hose	**tuubbo; dhuun**
insecticide	**sunta cayayaanka**
ladder	**sallaan**
machine	**mishiin**
microscope	**weyneyso**
nail	**musbaar**
padlock	**quful**
paint	**rinji**
pickax	**garweyn**
plank	**loox dheer**
plastic	**caag**
rope	**xadhig**
rubber	**rabadh; goome**
rust	**daxal**
saw	**dawaar**
scissors	**maqas**
screw	**iskuruug; bool**
screwdriver	**dismis**
sewing machine	**harqaan**
spade	**badeel**
spanner	**kiyaawo; baanad**
string	**xadhig dhuuban**
telescope	**diiradda xiddigiska**
wire	**waayir; fiilo; silig**

25. THE CAR

Driving — Unless you already know the country well, it is inadvisable to bring your own vehicle to Somalia. If you do, you will need an international driving license, car registration papers and insurance. It is unlikely you will find spare parts. Driving conditions were never optimal and the recent conflicts have taken a predictable toll on the road system.

Where can I rent a car?	**Halkee baan gaadhi ka kireysan karaa?**
Where can I rent a car with a driver?	**Halkee baan gaadhi iyo wadihiisa ka kiraysan karaa?**
How much is it per day?	**Maalintii kiradu waa immisa?**
How much is it per week?	**Wiiggii*/todobaadkii* kiradu waa immisa?**
Can I park here?	**Halkan gaadhiga ma dhigan karaa?**
Are we on the right road for . . . ?	**Ma ku taagannahay waddadii saxa ahayd ee . . . ?**
Where is the nearest filling station?	**Halkee ugu dhaw baadroole?**
Fill the tank please. normal/diesel	**Fadlan taangiga ii buuxi. caadi/naafto**
Check the oil/tires/ battery, please.	**Jeeggaree saliidda/ shaagagga/beyteriga.**
I've broken down.	**Gaadhigu wuu iga jabay.**
I have a puncture.	**Shaag ayaa iga banjaray.**
I have run out of gas.	**Batroolkii ayaa iga dhamaaday.**
Our car is stuck.	**Baabuurkaannu wunlimmaday.**

* Both mean 'week.'

There's something wrong with this car.	**Gaadhigan wax baa ka khaldan.**
We need a mechanic.	**Makaanig ayaanu u baahannahay.**
Where is the nearest garage?	**Mee geerashka halkan ugu dhawi?**
Can you tow us?	**Mana jiidi kartaa?**
Can you jump-start the car?	**Gaadhiga ma noo jugeyn kartaa?**
There's been an accident.	**Shil baabuur baa dhacay.**
My car has been stolen.	**Gaadhigaygii ayaa la xaday.**
Call the police!	**Booliiska u yeedh!**
driver's license	**liisan**
insurance policy	**inshooran; caymis**
car papers	**sharciga gaadhiga**
car registration	**diiwaan gelinta gaadhiga**

USEFUL WORDS

accelerator	**degdejiye**
air	**hawo**
anti-freeze	**ka hortagga biyo barafowga**
battery	**beytari**
bonnet	**kawar**
brake	**joojiye; bireeg**
bumper	**turus**
car park	**meel baabuurrada laadhigto**
clutch	**kileesh**
driver	**wade; dareewal**
engine	**ijiin; mishiin**
exhaust	**igsaas**
fan belt	**badhah**
gear	**geer; isbiidh**
indicator light	**bidhbidho**
inner-tube	**tiyuub**

jack	**jag**
mechanic	**makaanig**
neutral drive	**khali**
oil	**saliid**
oilcan	**qasacad saliid ah**
passenger	**rakaab**
petrol	**badrool**
radiator	**tangiga biyaha**
reverse	**reefas**
seat	**kursi**
spare tire	**taayirka/shaagga dheeraad ah**
speed	**isbiidh**
steering wheel	**shookaan**
tank	**taangi**
tire	**shaag**
tow rope	**xadhigga jiidista**
windscreen	**muraayadda hore**

26. COLORS

black	**madow**
blue	**buluug**
brown	**midab boodhe**
green	**cagaaran; doogo**
orange	**laymuuni**
red	**cas**
white	**cad**
yellow	**hurdi**

27. SPORTS

athletics	**ciyaaraha fudud**
ball	**kubbad**
basketball	**kubadda kolayga**
chess	**jas**
goal	**gool**
horse racing	**tartanka fardaha**
horse-riding	**fardo fuulid**
match	**ciyaar/dheel**
soccer match	**ciyaar kubadda cagta ah;**
	dheel kubadda cagta ah
pitch	**garoon**
rugby	**rugbi**
soccer	**kubadda cagta**
stadium	**staadiyum**
swimming	**dabbaal**
team	**tiim; koox**
wrestling	**legdin**
Who won?	**Yaa guuleystey?**
What's the score?	**Immisa gool baa dhashay?**

28. THE BODY

ankle	**canqow**
arm	**gacan**
back	**dhabar**
beard	**gadh**
blood	**dhiig**
body	**jidh**
bone	**laf**
bottom *informal*	**badhi**
breast	**naas**
chest	**xabbad**
chin	**gar**
ear	**dheg**
elbow	**suxul**
eye	**il**
face	**weji**
finger	**far**
foot	**cag**
genitals	**saxaax**
hair	**timo**
hand	**gacan**
head	**madax**
heart	**wadne**
jaw	**daan**
kidney	**keli**
kidneys	**kelyo**
knee	**jilib**
leg	**lug**
lip	**dibin**
liver	**beer**
lung	**sambab**
lungs	**sambabo**
moustache	**shaaruubo**
mouth	**af**
neck	**qoor**

nose	**san**
shoulder	**garab**
stomach	**calool**
throat	**cune**
thumb	**suul**
toe	**far cageed**
tongue	**carrab**
tooth	**ilig**
teeth	**ilko**
vein	**halbawle**
veins	**halbawleyaal**
womb	**min**
wrist	**jalaqley**

29. POLITICS

aid worker	**hawl wadeen hay'ad samofal**
ambassador	**danjire**
arrest	**xidh**
assassination	**shirqool**
assembly	**gole; guddi**
autonomy	**ismaamul**
cabinet	**golaha wasiirada**
a charity	**samafal; urur samafal ah**
citizen	**wadani/muwaaddin**
civil rights	**xuquuqda dadka**
civil war	**dagaal sokeeye**
communism	**shuucinimo**
communist	**shuuci**
constitution	**qaanuun; dastuur**
convoy	**kolanyo**
corruption	**musuq maasuq**
coup d'état	**afgembi**
crime	**dambi**
criminal	**dambiile**
crisis	**qalalaaso**
dictator	**keli taliye**
debt	**amaah**
democracy	**dimuqraadiyad**
dictatorship	**keli talisnimo**
diplomatic ties	**xidhiid dibloomaasi**
election	**doorasho**
embassy	**safaarad**
ethnic cleansing	**takoorid**
exile	**masaafur**
free	**xor**
freedom	**xoriyad**
government	**dawlad**
guerrilla	**dagaalyahan**
hostage	**afduubane**

humanitarian aid	**gargaar samofal ah**
human rights	**xuquuqal insaan**
imam	**iimaam**
independence	**madax bannaani**
independent	**madax bannaan**
independent state	**dal madax bannaan**
judge	**garsoore**
killer	**dilaa**
law court	**maxkamad sharci ah**
law	**sharci**
lawyer	**looyar; garyaqaan**
leader	**hoggaamiye**
left-wing	**garabka bidixda**
liberation	**xorayn**
majority	**inta badan; badnaan**
mercenary	**caloosha u shaqayste**
minister	**wasiir**
ministry	**wasaarad**
minority	**tirada yar**
murder	**gacan ku dhiigle**
opposition	**mucaarad**
parliament	**baarlamaan**
(political) party	**xisbi siyaasi ah**
politics	**siyaasad**
peace	**nabad**
peace-keeping troops	**ciidamada nabad ilaalinta**
politician	**siyaasi**
premier	**ra'iisal-wasaare**
president	**madaxweyne**
presidential guard	**ilaalada madaxweynaha**
prime minister	**ra'iisal-wasaare**
prison	**jeel; xabsi**
prisoner-of-war	**maxbuus dagaal**
POW camp	**xerada maxaabiista dagaalka**
protest	**diidmo**
rape	**kufsi**

reactionary	**dibusocod ah**
Red Cross	**Laanqayrta Cas**
refugee	**qaxooti**
revolution	**kacaan**
right-wing	**garabka midig**
robbery	**boob**
seat (in assembly)	**kursi; fadhi**
secret police	**booliiska sirta ah**
socialism	**hanti wadaagnimo**
socialist	**hanti wadaag**
spy	**basaas**
struggle	**halgan**
theft	**xatooyo**
trade union	**urur shaqaale**
treasury	**khasnad**
United Nations	**Qaraamada Midoobay**
veto	**fiito; codka diidmada qayaxan**
vote	**codbixin; food**
vote-rigging	**aadanyabaaleys**
voting	**codbixin**

30. TIME & DATES

century	**qarni**
decade	**toban guuro**
year	**sanad**
month	**bil**
fortnight	**laba toddobaad**
week	**wiig; toddobaad**
day	**maalin**
hour	**saacad**
minute	**miridh**
second	**seken; ilbiriqsi**
dawn	**salaad hore**
sunrise	**waaberi**
morning	**subax**
day	**maalin**
noon	**duhur**
afternoon	**galab**
evening	**caways**
sunset	**cadceed dhal**
night	**habeen**
midnight	**saqdhexe**
four days before	**afar cisho ka hor**
three days before	**saddex cisho ka hor**
the day before yesterday	**dorraad**
yesterday	**shalay**
last night	**xalay**
today	**maanta**
tomorrow	**berrito**
the day after tomorrow	**saa dambe**
three days from now	**saddex cisho maanta laga bilaabo**
four days from now	**afar cisho maanta laga bilaabo**

the year before last	**kal hore sanad ka hor**
last year	**kal-hore**
this year	**sanadkan**
next year	**sanadka dambe**
the year after next	**sanadka soo socda; sanad kedib**
last week	**wiiggii ina dhaafay**
this week	**wiiggan**
next week	**wiigga dambe**
this morning	**saakadan**
now	**imminka**
tonight	**caawa**
yesterday morning	**shalay subax**
yesterday afternoon	**shalay galab**
yesterday night	**xalay**
tomorrow morning	**berri subax**
tomorrow afternoon	**berri galab**
tomorrow night	**habeen dambe**
in the morning	**subaxdii**
in the afternoon	**galabtii**
in the evening	**cawayskii**
past	**xilli tegey**
present	**xilli jooga**
future	**xilli soo socda**
What date is it today?	**Maanta maalintu waa maalintee?**
What time is it?	**Waa immisadii?**
It is . . . o'clock.	**Waa . . . subaxnimo/ galabnimo/habeennimo.***

* In the morning/in the afternoon/in the evening.

DAYS OF THE WEEK

Monday	**isniin**
Tuesday	**salaasa**
Wednesday	**arbaca**
Thursday	**khamiis**
Friday	**jimce**
Saturday	**sabti**
Sunday	**axad**

MONTHS*

January	**Jeenawery; Janaayo**
February	**Feebarwery; Febraayo**
March	**Maarij; Maarso**
April	**Abriil**
May	**Meey; Maajo**
June	**Juun**
July	**Juulaay; Luulyo**
August	**Ogos; Agoosto**
September	**Sibtambar; Sebtember**
October	**Oktoobar**
November	**Noofembar**
December	**Diisembar**

* Where there are two variants, the first has come through English and the second through Italian.

31. NUMBERS & AMOUNTS

NOTE ON 'ONE': The numeral used in counting is **kow** — as listed below. However, when a noun follows, **hal** is used, e.g. **hal buug** 'one book.' When one particular thing is referred to then **mid** is used, e.g. **mid bay cuneen** 'they ate one.' Note that **koob** is also used in number combinations using 'one', e.g. 'eleven' is <u>**koob**</u> **iyo toban** as well as <u>**kow**</u> **iyo toban**

0	eber
1	kow
2	laba
3	saddex
4	afar
5	shan
6	lix
7	toddoba
8	siddeed
9	sagaal
10	toban
11	kow iyo toban; koob iyo toban
12	laba iyo toban
13	saddex iyo toban
14	afar iyo toban
15	shan iyo toban
16	lix iyo toban
17	toddoba iyo toban
18	siddeed iyo toban
19	sagaal iyo toban
20	labaatan
22	laba iyo labaatan
30	soddon
32	laba iyo soddon
40	afartan
42	laba iyo afartan
50	konton
52	laba iyo konton

60	**lixdan**
62	**laba iyo lixdan**
70	**toddobaatan**
72	**laba iyo toddobaatan**
80	**siddeetan**
82	**laba iyo siddeetan**
90	**sagaashan**
92	**laba iyo sagaashan**
100	**boqol**
102	**laba iyo boqol**
112	**boqol iyo laba iyo toban**
200	**laba boqol**
300	**saddex boqol**
400	**afar boqol**
500	**shan boqol**
600	**lix boqol**
700	**toddoba boqol**
800	**siddeed boqol**
900	**sagaal boqol**
1,000	**kun**
10,000	**toban kun**
50,000	**konton kun**
100,000	**boqol kun**
1,000,000	**malyuun**

first	**kowaad**
second	**labaad**
third	**saddexaad**
fourth	**afraad**
fifth	**shanaad**
tenth	**tobnaad**
fifteenth	**shaniyo tobnaad**
twentieth	**labaatanaad**

once	**mar**
twice	**laba jeer**

three times	**saddex jeer**
one-half	**badh**
one-quarter	**rubuc**
three-quarters	**saddex rubuc**
one-third	**hal saddex loo qaybiyey meel**
two-thirds	**laba saddex meelood loo qaybiyey meel**

32. WEIGHTS & MEASURES

kilometer	**kiiloomitir**
meter	**mitir**
mile	**mayl**
foot	**fuudh**
yard	**waar**
gallon	**galaan**
liter	**litir**
kilogram	**kiiloogaram**
gram	**garam**
pound	**rodol**
ounce	**wiqiyad**

33. OPPOSITES

beginning – end	**bilaw – dhamaad**
clean – dirty	**nadiif – uskag**
comfortable – uncomfortable	**raaxo ku ah – aan raaxo ku ahayn**
fertile – barren	**bacrin – aan bacrin ahayn**
happy – unhappy	**faraxsan – aan faraxsanayn**
life – death	**nolol – dhimasho**
friend – enemy	**saaxiib – cadaw; col**
modern – traditional	**casri – soo jireen; dhaqan ahaan**
modern – ancient	**casri – qaadiim**
open – shut	**fur – xidh**
wide – narrow	**balaadhan – dhuuban**
high – low	**sare – hoose**
peace – violence/war	**nabad – dagaal**
polite – rude	**edebsan – edebdaran**
silence – noise	**aammus – buuqbadan**
cheap – expensive	**jaban – qaali**
hot/warm – cold/cool	**kulayl; diiran – qabaw**
health – disease	**caafimaad – cudur**
well – sick	**bed qaba – buka**
night – day	**habeen – maalin**
top – bottom	**kor – hoos**
backwards – forwards	**xagga dambe – xagga hore**
back – front	**dambe – hore**
dead – alive	**dhintay – nool**
near – far	**dhaw – fog**
left – right	**bidix – midig**
up – down	**kor – hoos**
yes – no	**haa – maya**
here – there	**halkan – halkaas**
soft – hard	**jilicsan – adag**
easy – difficult	**sahlan – dhib badan**
quick – slow	**dhaqso – tartiib**

OPPOSITES

big – small	**weyn – yar**
old – young	**duq – dhalin yar**
tall – short	**dheer – gaaban**
strong – weak	**xooggan – taagyar; taagdaran**
success – failure	**guul – guuldarro**
new – old	**cusub – gaboobay**
question – answer	**su'aal – jawaab**
safety – danger	**ammaan – khatar**
good – bad	**wacan; fiican – xun**
true – false	**run – been**
light – heavy	**fudud – culus**
light *noun* – dark *noun*	**iftiin – mugdi**
truth – lie	**run – been**

There is a large body of work in English and other European languages, especially Italian, written on most aspects of the Somali people, culture, language and land. The best — and most accessible — introduction to modern history currently available is *A Modern History of Somalia: Nation & State in the Horn of Africa* (Boulder, 1988) by Ioan Lewis. Providing an expert insight into how Somali society works, also by the same author, is *Blood & Bone: The Call of Kinship in Somali Society* (New Jersey, 1993). An excellent introduction to popular culture is *An Anthology of Somali Poetry* (Bloomington, 1993) by B. W. Andrzejewski with S. Andrzejewski. Soon to be published is *The Somalis: A Handbook* (Curzon Press, London). And highly recommended is any of the wide selection of works produced by Haan Associates, an organisation based in London which is dedicated to producing Somali-related materials.